Free
C.B.C.

THE
VATICAN
PICTURE
· BOOK · ·

A PICTURE
PILGRIMAGE

Edited by LEON PAUL

GREYSTONE PRESS - HAWTHORN BOOKS

All photos
Religious News Service

Art Work by Robert Rotter

Library of Congress Catalog Card Number 57-7688

NIHIL OBSTAT:
  Martinus S. Rushford, Ph.D.
IMPRIMATUR
  Eduardus P. Hoar, P.A., LL.D.
    Vicarius Capitularis Bruklyniensis
BRUKLYNII
  Die IV Decembris, 1956

Dedicated

to

THE CATHOLIC PARENTS

of

THE UNITED STATES

and CANADA

Whose Filial Love for

The Person of

The Holy Father

Has Been Frequently Demonstrated

And Is Affectionately

Handed Down From

Generation to Generation

of Catholic Children

· I N T R O D

THE UNQUENCHABLE hope of every Catholic is that some day, some how, in some unexpected way, it will become possible for him to visit Rome. To a Catholic, Rome is not merely another name of a city listed in travel folders that beckon you to Europe, where you will also find London, Paris, Amsterdam and Zurich...you know, the usual cities on a European itinerary. To a Catholic, the very sound of the name...*Rome*...brings forth echoes of a colorful and meaningful heritage, but most of all, Rome means *St. Peter's*, it means *The Vatican*, it means — the person who, above all persons, is most dear to every truly Catholic heart — *the Holy Father*.

From this, the smallest state in the world, the entire Church is directed and governed; from this heart of Catholicism flows the life blood which nourishes the members of the Mystical Body wherever they may be, in the farthest corners of the world. From *The Vatican* come the appointments of our Cardinals and Bishops, our Monsignori; from this citadel of learning come the many learned encyclicals and the many talks given by the Chief Shepherd to various members of his flock; from here also come new laws and regulations on the sacred liturgy, on the Eucharistic fast, on the Easter Vigil ...in fact, all that concerns Catholics in the world and life of today. From here also come the relics of the Saints for patronal churches, shrines and for individuals. It would be a monumental task to list all the benefits and blessings which flow like a mighty river to all the corners of the world, from the *Vatican*, and from the person of *Our Holy Father*.

UCTION·

To a Catholic, the pope *is* a father, a Holy Father, the head of the entire Catholic family — nations, peoples, parishes and families. The hope to see the Holy Father in person and obtain his blessing is certainly in the heart of every Catholic, but it is not always within the realm of possibility for everyone to accomplish this. Too many obstacles stand in the way of most of us...

Even various parts of Europe would be a considerable journey to Rome. Pilgrims from *Dublin, Glasgow, London, Brussels, Paris* or *Lisbon* would still have to travel long distances and many days to reach the Eternal City...How much more difficult would it be then, for pilgrims from *Los Angeles, Chicago, New York, New Orleans, Montreal* or *Boston?* For all of these loom over 4,000 miles of turbulent, restless ocean and for many, additional thousands of miles of mountains, prairies and highways. These are only some of the seemingly impossible obstacles for many who would like to visit Rome. Some fortunate few among us are able to make it, but for most of us, family obligations, our jobs or a budget that simply refuses to stretch out some 7,000 miles, prevents us from making this pilgrimage...

Why not then a *"Picture Pilgrimage...?"* Why not visit Rome from our own homes, visually and spiritually? This is just what we have attempted to do here. We have put together, not an album of beautiful photographs alone, but have chosen those particular pictures which would help us to make our pilgrimage with reverence, to see in these pictures not so much the *"here's a good shot..."* aspect, but to look upon these scenes and events with the eyes of faith, to look upon the various ceremonies and people as though we were actually kneeling in St. Peter's, or watching Our Holy Father in his various activities, or seeing something that others may have missed...

This VATICAN PICTURE BOOK is an attempt at just such an approach... an attempt to make this a spiritual pilgrimage that will take you across the thousands of miles of land and sea in one fell swoop and put you *in* The Vatican, *in* St. Peter's and in the presence of the *Chief Shepherd of Rome* so that you can see them with your own eyes, and enjoy them and be inspired by them as if you were actually there. Look upon each scene with the eyes of your heart, the eyes of your mind, the eyes — *of your soul ...!*

It is our earnest prayer that until the time comes, when the providence of God makes it possible for you to see and enjoy all these things in actuality — in all their indescribable color, magnificence and glory — you may meanwhile benefit from and enjoy this spiritual pilgrimage, this *"Picture Pilgrimage"* if you will, which you can make any time at your convenience, whenever and as often as you wish...

If you want to drop us a note or a card letting us know how you liked this *"Picture Pilgrimage"* we certainly would enjoy hearing from you...

Now — let's get going ... we've delayed long enough!

Leon Paul

OUR
PILGRIMAGE
BEGINS... ◇ ◇ ◇

Our plans for going to Rome have been completed. We try to visualize all the things that have become familiar to us—*St. Peter's Square* with the great Basilica towering beyond it...the *Vatican Palace*...*Our Holy Father himself*...the colorful and handsome Swiss Guards...Michelangelo's *"Pieta"*...the *Sistine Chapel* and all the many other things that we can hardly wait to see...

Yet, while we are going to see many of the *"sights"* in the Vatican, and in the Eternal City, we want to approach these sacred places in a spirit of prayer. We want to look upon them, not so much as sightseers, but as *pilgrims*, seeing these shrines and masterpieces, these buildings and rooms and sacred tombs of the Saints—as the pilgrims of old had done, and still do—with the eyes of faith... not curiosity!...

In all these things we shall see the greatness and the goodness and the glory of God, remembering that it was for His Glory that all these things were built, and painted and sculptured...and it was for His Truth that the Saints who were martyred here, willingly gave their lives...We would be poor Catholics indeed, who did not see the finger of God, and the love of God, and the goodness of God —in all these things...

We are approaching Rome by plane. It is easy to pick out many landmarks that have become familiar to us. Our pilot deliberately flies in low over *St. Peter's* to give us a breathtaking view of the great Basilica and of all of Vatican City...It is a view—and a sight—we shall always treasure... *our first view of The Vatican...* *and St. Peter's...*

After landing at *Ciampino* field near the *Via Appia,* a bus takes us to our hotel not far from St. Peter's. We unpack, have our dinner and relax for the evening for we have a big day ahead of us tomorrow.

Very early the next morning, we make our way to the Vatican and to the office of *Eugene Cardinal Tisserant,* in the Palazo dei Convertendi, on the Piazza S. Callisto. A priest friend of ours back home had written to His Eminence and made the appointment for us.

Cardinal Tisserant, Dean of the College of Cardinals and Secretary of the Sacred Congregation for the Oriental Church, has kindly consented to help us on our pilgrimage. He was most gracious and spoke about our mutual friend, our diocese and our bishop. He had arranged with a young priest who knows the Vatican thoroughly, to be our guide. The priest joined us a few minutes after we arrived at the Cardinal's office. We were introduced and His Eminence suggested that we begin our pilgrimage by attending Mass which was soon to be celebrated by *Our Holy Father himself* for an American group in one of the private chapels in The Vatican, the *Sala Ducale.*

We thanked His Eminence, kissed his ring, and left with our guide. On the way to the chapel, the young priest told us that Cardinal Tisserant was also the president of the *Pontifical Commission of Biblical Studies* instituted by Pope Leo XIII. He is also the Prefect of the *Sacred Congregation of Ceremonies.* We asked where he comes from. He was born in Nancy, France in 1884 (on March 4th). He was ordained in 1907 and created a Cardinal on June 15th, 1936.

We were certainly impressed with our short visit to Cardinal Tisserant, especially with his friendliness and humility... We were at the entrance to the Chapel now, and went in...

A fairly large crowd already filled the *Sala Ducale* chapel. Soon, the small procession came out of the sacristy and we got our first glimpse of *Pope Pius XII!* We have been to Mass many times, for many years, in our parish church, even in other cities. But never before have we been at Mass celebrated by Our Holy Father himself! This was indeed a thrilling and a most unforgettable experience!

We noticed the various uniforms of the Noble Guards standing on each side of the altar and on either side of the chapel. On the right side, between two of the Swiss Guards, we noticed something that gave us another thrill. Here, in the heart of the Eternal City, and at a Mass celebrated by the Supreme Pontiff himself, stood an American flag! What a wonderful thing it was to see it —here!

We prayed for special blessings upon our flag, our country and all our people, especially the poor, the sick, the unemployed and all those in need...we prayed for our President and all those in authority, that they might lead their people closer to God...and bring God closer to their people ...we prayed especially for all the school-children of America ... for American families...Catholic Action and the Lay Apostolate... and many other things...

After Mass, we had breakfast. Afterwards we made our way up toward the great dome of St. Peter's. On the way, we stopped to see the *"Big Bell"* of St. Peter's which is located under one of the clocks. Our guide told us it weighed about 10 tons! I was hoping it wouldn't ring while we were so close to it... but our priest friend told us that it is only rung on special occasions. It's loud,, booming peals signalled the opening of the Holy Year in 1950, and was soon joined by all the bells of St. Peter's. This huge bell is also tolled when there is a canonization... and on other very special occasions.

Meanwhile we got a good view of *St. Peter's Square* and the surrounding area. Our guide pointed out some of the many famous landmarks and points of interest . . . especially other Roman churches and many Catholic colleges.

We then proceeded toward the huge dome... *Michelangelo's Dome!*

A few elevator rides and many flights of stairs later, we reached the area of the great dome. The tip of the cross is 452 feet above ground! The *Statue of Liberty*, with its base and all, could easily fit INSIDE St. Peter's and clear the top of the dome with almost 100 feet to spare! Our priest-guide pointed out many of the buildings inside Vatican City; the Railroad Station, the Governor's Palace, the Old Observatory, the Ethiopian College, the Sistine Chapel, the Old Gardens and many other things...what a magnificent view!

While we were there, seven steeple-jacks — or *Sampietrini*, as they are called here—climbed skillfully up to the top from ladder to ladder. They were making preparations for the lighting of the great dome for a demonstration by 250,000 young men belonging to Italian Catholic Action who were coming to The Vatican to manifest their loyalty to the Holy Father.

Our guide said that for such an occasion, it requires the services of 500 Sampietrini to prepare St. Peter's for an electrical display of its beauty. He also told us that 16 people could fit inside that ball up there, if anyone wanted to try it...but none of us did.

Our priest glanced at his watch. *"It's time to be getting down,"* he said, *"I want you to get a good close view of the Changing of the Guard in Belvedere Courtyard..."*

On the way down, he briefed us on the Swiss Guards, perhaps the best known and most colorful of the Vatican's Police Department. They were founded in 1505, thirteen years after Columbus discovered America. A Swiss Cardinal made a treaty with Pope Julius II promising to supply 250 men as a Papal bodyguard. Only native Swiss young men may join the corps; they must be bachelors, 5 feet 8 inches tall, and in perfect physical health.

When the Pope is carried on the *Sedia Gestatoria*, his portable throne, he is surrounded by six amour-clad Swiss Guardsmen. When Rome was sacked in 1527, almost two hundred of these Swiss Guards were killed while helping Pope Clement VII to reach the safety of *Castel Sant'Angelo...*

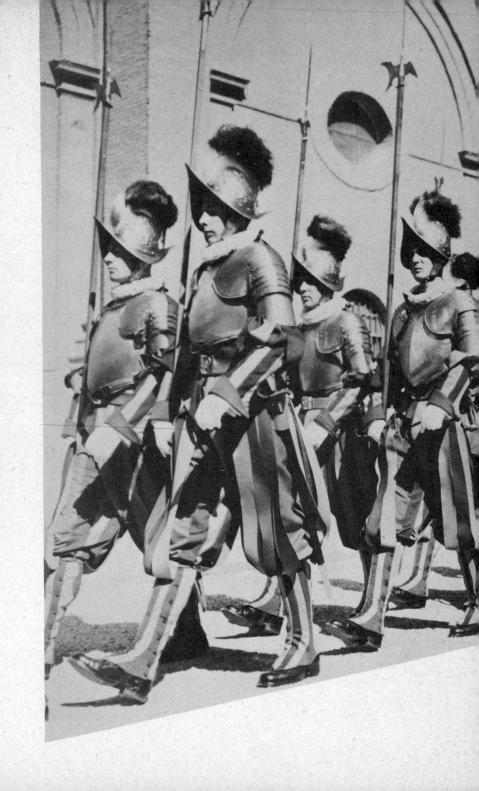

In perhaps the most colorful military uniforms in all the world, the *Swiss Guards* make an impressive sight with their blue, red and yellow outfits, their shining silver breastplates and helmets. Because of the long-shafted weapon they carry, called *"halberds"* they are known as *"halberdiers."* Michelangelo or Raphael is said to have designed their picturesque medieval uniforms, *"The Army of the Pope"* is a dedicated and happy combination of soldiers and monks where many of the features of each life are placed at the service of the Chief Shepherd of Rome. They make a thrilling sight...!

The beatification ceremony for an American nun was scheduled to begin in half an hour, so we went inside St. Peter's to get as near the papal throne as we could...

Before very long, the Holy Father came out and sat below a colorful, religious tapestry. He was flanked by cardinals, bishops and members of the nobility, as well as members of the Noble Guard, one of whom stood on our right on the steps. Swiss Guards and other members of the Vatican household stood in front of us.

The Holy Father was clad in magnificent golden vestments and a gold mitre. A group of priests and bishops stood before him giving the peroration for the beatification of this particular American nun, the foundress of a religious order. The Holy Father listened with marked interest.

After the ceremony, the Supreme Pontiff was carried on the *Sedia Gestatoria* through St. Peter's to pontificate at another ceremony that was to take place. His energy seems inexhaustible! He made a beautiful sight as he was carried through the historic basilica blessing the people as he passed by, some people applauded, others cheered him as he passed..."*Viva il Papa!* ...*Viva il Papa!*"

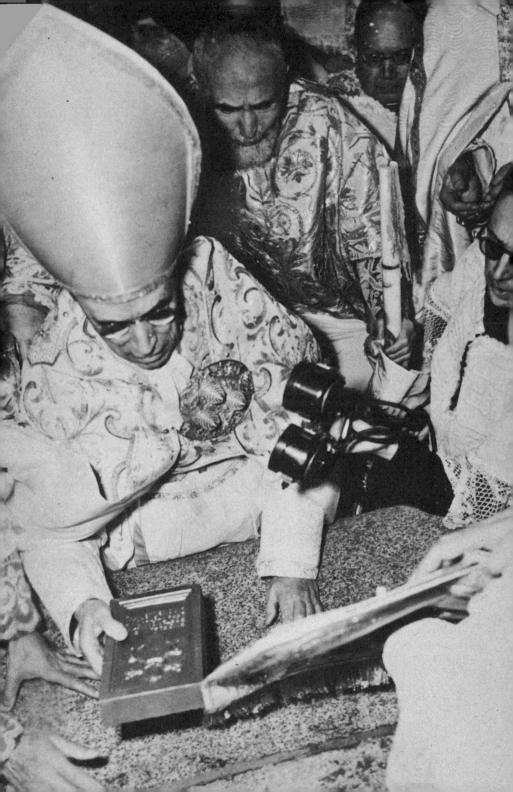

The young priest who was our guide was evidently very familiar with St. Peter's. He knew just where to take us for each ceremony we were to attend, so that we could see everything perfectly. This time, he took us to a vantage point right in front of where the Holy Father was going to perform the ceremony...which was to be broadcast according to all the microphones everywhere.

We got our closest view of our beloved Pope clad now in vestments of silver and gold brocade and a jewel-studded mitre. His voice during the prayers was strong, clear and inspiring!

We were absolutely surrounded by cardinals, bishops, monsignori and Swiss Guards.

After this ceremony, the Holy Father was carried away again, and slowly, the huge crowd dispersed. Our guide told us that the tomb of *Maria Goretti* was on view and asked us if we would like to see her. We had heard so much about this young child who was killed protecting herself against the unchaste desires of a farm-hand, and in fact had some devotion to the young Saint after she was canonized during the Holy Year in 1950...

We were certainly anxious to see her tomb and our guide happily led the way...

Maria Goretti was an innocent child of 12 when Alexander Serenelli, a 17 year old farmhand in *Nettuno*, southern Italy, caught her and demanded something that Maria knew belonged to God alone. She resisted his advances and in his frustration and anger, Alexander killed her. As she lay dying on that hot July 6th in 1902, Maria forgave her murderer. But she kept her chastity and gave it back to God when her pure soul was called to Him later that day.

The *Passionists* were in charge of the parish church in Nettuno where Maria went to Mass. They took up her Cause, and wrote up all the papers that were needed to present Maria Goretti for beatification and later for canonization.

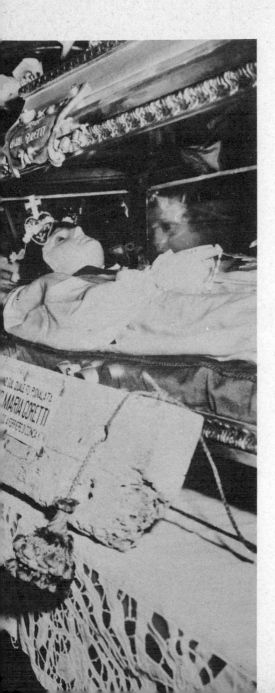

Alexander Serenelli went to prison for his crime, and when he came out on Christmas eve 1937 he immediately went to Mrs. Assunta Goretti to ask her pardon for killing Maria. *"If God has forgiven you,"* she said, *"and if Maria has forgiven you then I also forgive you."* He attended Midnight Mass with the Goretti family and received Communion with them. Then he went to a Capuchin monastery somewhere in Italy to do penance for his sins. He did not become a Capuchin, but was merely allowed to live there as a Penitent ... and he is still there today ...

Our guide told us that Maria Goretti was declared a Saint on June 24th, 1950 during the Holy Year. Her feast day is on July 9th, the day on which she was killed. We noticed two lovely children in the group that came to venerate the relics, and we prayed to St. Maria Goretti, asking the young Saint to help little girls all over the world to remain pure and holy and to be pleasing to God, even if they have to give their lives—as she had done ...

Our priest-guide then told us that we could also venerate the relics of *Pope Pius X* who was recently declared a Saint. We wanted *very much* to see St. Pius X and again, our efficient guide led the way.

He told us that *Giuseppe Sarto* was born in Riese in 1835 and after he became a priest, was always humble, unostentatious, and kind, When he went to Rome for the papel election as Patriarch of Venice, he bought a round-trip ticket, never expecting to be elected himself! He became Pope on August 4th, 1903 *(one year after the martyrdom of Maria Goretti!)*

He died of a broken heart, caused by World War I, on August 20th, 1914, after a reign of 11 years. He was a great Pope for children, and instituted many reforms that would bring children closer to God, particularly the new law that made it possible for children to receive Communion as soon as they reached the age of reason—around seven years of age. And he encouraged frequent Communion, not only for children, but for all Catholics. Yes, we owe a great deal to this saintly Pontiff, and it was a great thrill, finally, when we stood before the bronze and crystal casket that held his remains. Pius X was canonized on May 29th, 1954. His feast day is on September 3rd...

A silver mask replica was over his face. His body was clothed in a white papal robe and a red ermine-edged cape, or *mozzetta*. He wore a papal ring over white gloves.

Swiss Guards stood watch before the relics which had been placed on a temporary altar in the great basilica. A beautiful painting of the Saintly Pope hung in a window in the background. We knelt in prayer before *St. Pius X* asking him for many favors, but especially for peace for the world...

Our guide then led us toward the *Altar of Confession*—the Main Altar in St. Peter's. Behind the altar was a marble balustrade. We walked through the opening into a sunken oval space and down two flights of steps. Many votive lamps attached to the balustrade made this whole area seem like hallowed ground—which indeed it was! Precious stones and sparkling jewels adorned the walls and

the floor. We were told that the votive lamps burn continually in honor of St. Peter, whose tomb was below.

We passed Canova's beautiful statue of *Pope Pius VI*, kneeling, his tiara beside him. Continuing down, we passed through ancient passageways, rooms and tombs. Finally we came to these archeological excavations which were ordered by Pope Pius XII to provide better spacing and arrangement for the tombs of Popes and Royal personages buried under the great church.

A major reason for these excavations was also to discover the existence and location of the tomb of a Jewish fisherman of Capharnaum, brother of Andrew . . . *Simon Bar-Jona,* who became the first Pope, *St. Peter the Apostle* in whose honor this great basilica had been built!

Looking around we noticed on the walls, crosses and prayers scratched there by pilgrims of the early centuries who came here to worship and to venerate the relics of St. Peter and the other popes and saints. We saw many ancient tombs like those on the right and in the center. Our guide translated many of the Latin inscriptions still readable on these early tombs of some of the very first Christians and martyrs . . . We said a silent prayer to them that if we ever have to die for our Faith, we might do so as bravely as they did . . . and we thought of the many thousands of Catholics in Russia, China, Poland, Hungary and those other countries under Communist domination, for whom martyrdom was no idle threat . . . May God give them strength and courage to endure their daily martyrdom for Christ . . . as these others did 17, 18 and 19 centuries ago . . .

By the time we came out, it was night. St. Peter's and The Vatican were aglow with thousands of lights that gave it the appearance of a tremendous sparkling jewel, resplendent against the velvety darkness of the Roman night sky. It was such an overwhelming sight that we just stood transfixed in St. Peter's Square looking at the various details we had seen in the daylight.

Our Holy Father's personal apartments on the third floor on the right were also lit up.

The huge Obelisk was a dark shaft silhoutted
against the myriad lights of the Basilica. As we
stood and watched, people flowed into the Square.
Altho we were quite tired, we decided to stay and
watch whatever was going to take place. After all,
you only see something like this once in a life-
time...! It was like a vision of heaven...and we
thanked God for making it possible for us to be
here...

Early the next morning we returned to St. Peter's and altho we were still impressed with the size of the basilica, everything seemed pale and gray compared to last night's dazzling nocturnal display, which someone said was like *"frozen fireworks."*

Our guide met us at the Obelisk as planned. He gave us a brief run-down on the things we saw and the place we stood. The Obelisk near which we stood originally came from *Heliopolis* and once stood in *Nero's Circus* over part of which St. Peter's now stands. The bronze cross at the top contains a relic of the True Cross!

Pope Julius II laid the foundation stone for the present basilica in 1506. Work continued under *Leo X* who appointed the youthful *Raphael* to work on it. In 1545, *Paul III* appointed *Michelangelo,* who was then 72 years old, to complete what others had begun. The great genius died in 1564 with the dome still unfinished. It was completed, finally in 1585; *Pope Sixtus V* ordered *Giacomo della Porta* and *Domenico Fontana* to complete the dome in the shortest possible time—whatever the cost . . .!

The Facade (the front of the basilica) was built in 1614 and twelve years later, *Pope Urban VIII* consecrated the finished church, the largest one in the entire world! It took 120 years to build and cost over a billion dollars! It is 700 feet long on the outside and from the pavement to the tip of the cross on the dome it is 452 feet high. "You can get the entire populations of the cities of Reno and Las Vegas, Nevada into St. Peter's," quipped our guide, "and it might do many of them good! The basilica holds or *can* hold, about 80,000 people. You certainly could get everyone in the city of Galveston, Texas into it, with only 66,568!"

There are 284 giant columns around the square in four rows, making three covered avenues on either side of the Square. The center aisle is wide enough for two autos to drive down side by side! The colonnades were erected by *Bernini* over 300 years ago under *Pope Alexander VII*. Above them on the balustrades, stand 164 giant statues! One stands on top of each outside column.

The *"big bell"* we saw before is just under the clock on the left...

We started our second day in the Holy City with Mass again, this time celebrated at the main altar, or the great *Altar of Confession* as it is called. Our Holy Father is the only one who ever says Mass at this altar, which was built directly over the tomb of St. Peter. Even *Constantine's Basilica* had the main altar on this very spot.

We were fortunate to get a place not too far from the altar and we could see everything very clearly. It was with great difficulty, however, that we concentrated on the Mass, distracted by *Bernini's* famous twisted columns, and the great baldacchino above, and the statues and altars all around us. Around the frieze below the dome, I could read part of the words to Our Lord to St. Peter: *"TU ES PETRUS ET SUPER HANC PETRAM AEDIFICABO ECCLESIAM MEAM ET TIBI DABO CLAVES REGNI COELORUM"* —*Thou art Peter and upon this rock I will build My Church and to thee I will give the keys of the Kingdom of Heaven.* Our guide told us later that these letters are six feet high!

At about the time of the Elevation of the Host and the Chalice, streams of light poured in from the beautiful stained glass windows making the sight one of almost heavenly beauty. Cardinals and bishops knelt on the side of the altar. Many priests and Religious were at this Mass, and thousands upon thousands of people. The Holy Father celebrates Mass *facing* the congregation...!

As I looked around *(which I shouldn't have been doing!)* I could only think of that phrase in the Lavabo psalm which we read during the Mass: *"...I have loved, O Lord, the beauty of Thy house, and the place where Thy glory dwelleth..."* I wonder if the Psalmist could possibly have seen a vision of Mass in St. Peter's when he wrote those words...?

After making his thanksgiving after Mass, Our Holy Father was carried on the *sedia gestatoria* through St. Peter's. From where we stood, we could see him most clearly as he passed, and in fact, had to move back out of the way of the *Noble Guard* who kept people from getting too close.

It was a wonderful feeling to be so close to the Vicar of Christ, to receive so many blessings from him. It was so typical of this Pope, he wanted to give people so much, of Christ, of himself, all the blessings it was possible to give people. His face and his smile showed forth his kindness, and his desire to give of himself; to help people to be happy, and good, and full of love for God and for one another.

I remarked to our priest-guide later that I thought this Pope was one of the *best* we ever had, and he agreed. He also thought that Pius XII was one of the *holiest* Popes we ever had, and wouldn't be surprised if he was canonized himself some day, like his predecessor, *Pius X*.

I mentioned that I had always had a deep regard for the previous Pope, *Pius XI*. I admired him tremendously for all the things that he did, the encyclicals he wrote, and the courage he showed on numerous occasions. Our guide said that Pius XII felt the same way about him and this was the reason he chose to carry on with the same name. Cardinal Pacelli was Secretary of State under Pius XI and had a better chance of knowing him than anyone else.

Mentioning Cardinal Pacelli reminded me of the time he visited the United States — the only pope ever to have done so — although of course, he was not pope at the time. But it must be good for him to have travelled so extensively while he was able to. Now he merely "*commutes*" between St. Peter's and Castel Gandolfo . . . !

Later, when the throne was set down, Our Holy Father began to receive some visitors. An Italian farmer knelt before him and presented the Pontiff with a replica of a Sicilian horse cart filled with fruit and vegetables. This was in honor of the new feast of *St. Joseph the Workman* which this Pope created recently to be celebrated on May 1st.

Pius XII spoke with the farmer for a little while and then presented him with a medallion of *St. Isadore,* patron saint of farmers. Following this the farmer kissed the papal ring and stepped back.

Then, microphones were moved in and Our Holy Father addressed a number of pilgrims who were members of the *Italian Association of Catholic Workers* gathered in Rome at this time to mark the organizations 10th anniversary.

Following this address—much applause and many shouts of *"Viva il Papa! Viva il Papa! Viva...!"*

When the shouting and the applause subsided, another group approached the Supreme Pontiff. As soon as he saw them, he got up from the throne and moved toward them . . .

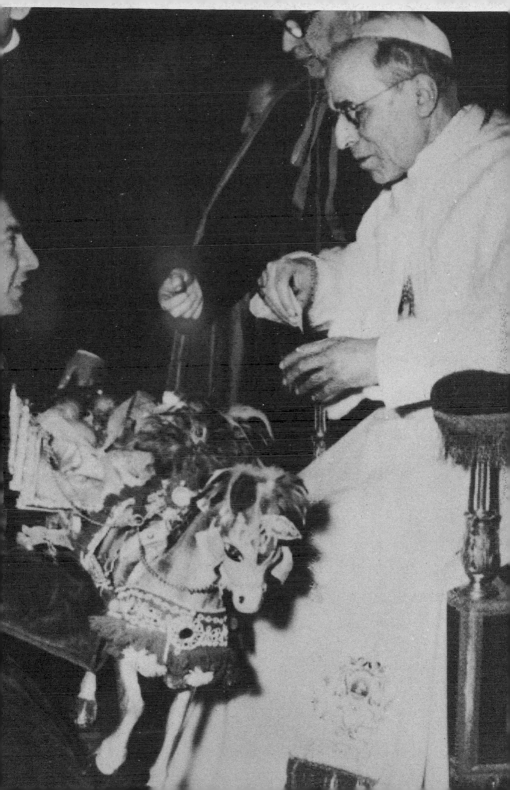

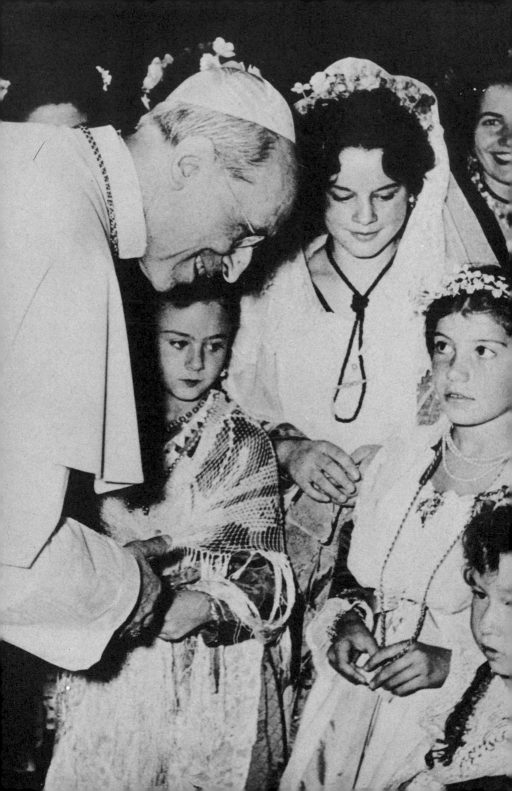

If there is any group that can capture the heart of this particular Pope, it is a group of children. Here were a group of girls in native costume who came to present their Holy Father with some choice fruit grown in their native Italian villages. This fruit had been blessed in the annual *"Blessing of the Peaches"* ceremony.

The little girl in front was presenting some of this fruit when, as sometimes happens, she *"forgot her lines!"* But the Holy Father, who is always mindful of the feelings of people and of children, noticed her embarrassment, and prompted her. He got a great deal of enjoyment out of the entire thing, and he finally got the little girl to smile. He gave each one a medal which he had blessed.

The Pope's interest in children is universal. It was he who canonized *Maria Goretti*, patroness of girls, and *Dominic Savio*, patron of youth. The children of the world owe a tremendous debt to this great Holy Father— a Holy Father in the truest sense of the name ...! It was a wonderful thing to watch him as he spoke to these children. Although they looked at him sometimes, with awe and wonder, he made them quite at ease after only a few moments in his presence.

I'll bet he wishes that he had the time to read stories to them or even participate in some of their games, if his great position permitted him to ... But that's the kind of priest this Holy Father seems to be.

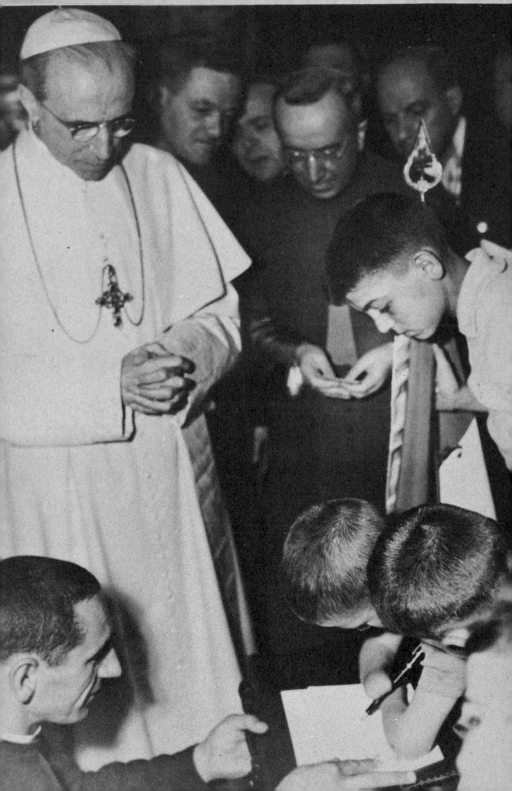

Another group waiting for the Holy Father's visit was a group of about 150 crippled children who had been maimed and mutilated in the last war. One poor little kid who lost both hands demonstrates his ability to overcome his terrible handicap by writing something with the little stubs of his arms.

The Pontiff stood by and watched intently. He was very much affected by these children and it showed in his face. The priest showed the boy's writing to the Holy Father, who read it aloud: *"...long live the Pope!"*

I almost thought he was going to cry, he was so moved by all this. But he placed his hands upon the boy's head and blessed him. Then he asked him his name and other questions, and told him to trust in God and to have courage. He spoke to each of the children and blessed each one of them.

Then he turned to the grown-ups there, the priests and laymen who accompanied the children. The Supreme Pontiff recalled the love of Christ for children and expressed the certainty that generous souls would never be wanting so that children like these can be given lives of usefulness, happiness and peace in spite of—and even *because* of, their handicaps...

Our Holy Father moved on, to another group waiting for him in one of the next audience chambers. These were members of the *Third Order of St. Francis*. In the true tradition of the gentle Saint who called all the animals his brothers, these *Tertiaries* presented His Holiness with a pair of small doves.

I believe that Our Holy Father is himself a member of the *Third Order of St. Francis* and also loves animals. He is the first Pope to keep pets in the Vatican apartments. He has a number of caged canaries, one of which —a very tame *"Cathedral Singer"*— he is very fond of. In the summertime, he even takes them to Castel Gandolfo with him.

We got quite a kick out of the little boy who couldn't see and peeked around the Holy Father for a better look. When the Pontiff saw him, he turned around, and stooping over, showed the boy the doves. An assistant held the birds while the Holy Father addressed the group briefly on the spirit of St. Francis living in the world today and doing the good that he would do, through the members of his Third Order. Then they all knelt down for the Papal Blessing, and while they shouted *"Viva il Papa... Viva il Papa"* he made his way to another audience-chamber...

This time, a delegation of *American Boy Scouts* were waiting to see the Holy Father. They sang some Boy Scout hymns and recited the Scout Oath for him. The Pontiff asked one of the boys where they were from, who the bishop of their diocese was, and a few other questions about Scouting. He asked another boy where they were going. The scout told His Holiness that they were on their way to a *World Scout Jamboree* in Austria.

Once again, the Holy Father showed his interest in youth and spoke to these scouts on the importance of remaining faithful to their Scout promises, and to the Scout Oath. He also told them that it was important for them to be good Catholics as well as good Scouts. No boy can be a true scout, he reminded them, unless he is true to his religious duties...

The scouts knelt for the Holy Father's blessing, and as the Supreme Pontiff left the audience-chamber, he was pleased to hear some well-rehearsed Scout cheers in the American idiom.

In still another audience-chamber, a small boatload of sailors from the *Mediterranean fleet* were waiting anxiously and nervously, for a visit from the Pope. They were a spectacle of white against the deep colors of the paintings and tapestries of the room. When the Holy Father entered, it was immediately noticeable that his white cassock blended perfectly with their white uniforms.

He passed from one to the other, asking their names, home towns, who their bishop was and asked them to convey his regards to each one's bishop. They all had handfulls of rosaries which they asked the Pontiff to bless and he did so graciously. He spoke to each one warmly and it was evident that he was interested in their welfare. It was like a father speaking to his sons — as indeed it was!

During World War II, the Holy Father granted audiences to many thousands of soldiers, sailors, marines, chaplains, any of them who would come to *The Vatican*, he would see, and bless. He often spoke of his great love and admiration for the heroic young men who fought to save the world from Naziism, and other evils that sought to enslave entire peoples...

His gratitude to the men who serve their country is evident whenever he finds servicemen in an audience. The *Pope of Peace* is the Father, the Spiritual Father of men who go to war — and he has helped countless servicemen to find peace in the midst of war...and between wars...

Just before six o'clock, the Holy Father went to a small chapel where Msgr. Domenico Tardini, Vatican *Pro-Secretary of State* was waiting with a few of the orphan boys from his *Villa Nazareth*. Promptly at six, bells began to ring and the Holy Father began the Angelus... *"The Angel of the Lord declared unto Mary..."* and we all responded... *"And she conceived by the Holy Ghost..."*

It was a wonderful privilege to says the Angelus with the Supreme Pontiff himself! And it was pleasant to listen to the children as they joined in the responses. Msgr. Tardini knelt just to Our Holy Father's right, behind one of his boys. After the Angelus, Pope Pius spoke with the boys, asked them how they were getting on at the Villa, and after a few words with Msgr. Tardini and the others, he left for his own private chapel for some undisturbed prayer before the Blessed Sacrament. He always spends some time in the chapel before dinner, which, by the way, he always eats alone.

Later on, after we left the Vatican, our priest-guide told us something about this Villa Nazareth... which Msgr. Tardini founded in Easter 1946...a home for orphan boys that was certainly original, even unique, and very much needed.

Villa Nazareth will accept boys who are either orphans, or from poverty-stricken homes; they must be about 5 years old; have above-average intelligence and be physically fit. The whole idea was to save these children from being ruined or wasting their lives as delinquents. Only 60 boys could be accommodated. But they would be given every opportunity of using their talents in art, music, education, medicine, etc. They are taught by *Sisters of Charity,* 8 lay teachers, a doctor, a nurse, a physical-education director, music and art teachers...

Every afternoon, when he is finished with the multitudinous affairs of state, Monsignor Tardini begins the half-hour trip to Villa Nazareth on a hill overlooking St. Peter's. The boys wait for him as children wait for their father... and no father loves his children more than Msgr. Tardini loves his orphans. No doubt, when these lads grow up and go out into the world for which the Villa Nazareth has prepared them — they will put to the best possible advantage, the gifts and the talents nurtured and perfected by Msgr. Tardini's foresight and vision. And they will thank God for men like — Monsignor Tardini... *the Don Bosco of the Vatican!*

After dinner, we were invited to a demonstration of TV. The Catholics of France were presenting a television set to the Supreme Pontiff. *Count Wladimir D'Ormesson*, French Ambassador to The Vatican made the presentation. The Count was colorfully beribboned and decorated—he must have been wearing at least a dozen medals on his embroidered military-looking jacket.

Our Holy Father seemed to be enjoying it all. He admitted to being a frustrated TV fan recently, when he granted an audience to the contestants of *"Double or Quits"* a popular TV show in Italy. The Pontiff said that he was almost always too busy to watch TV as much as he would like, although he now has sets at both Castel Gandolfo and in his Vatican apartment. He said that most of what he knows about quiz programs he learns from the newspapers where TV is often front page news.

I was tempted to ask Our Holy Father if he ever watches Bishop Sheen on TV...he would enjoy the bishop's *Life Is Worth Living*...

By the time we left, night had wrapped Rome into its vast bosomy darkness and the myriad stars twinkled like sequins on its draped mantle while the magnificent dome of St. Peter's shone through the night like a crown of light and beauty and grace...

Statues of saints and apostles stood silhouetted against the huge, brightly lit dome as if they were so many sentinels guarding the most precious crown of a king... and the dome does remind me of a crown, with its graceful, sculptured lines, and upon its crest, a golden ball supporting the symbol of our Faith — *the Cross*...

Even seeing this mighty dome with my own eyes it was difficult to believe that it was so tremendous. Imagine 16 people in that small ball near the summit!...

Just as the stately white dome of the *Sacre Coeur* overlooking all of Paris — so also, the massive dome of St. Peter's stood over all of Rome, a Guardian watching over its children by day and by night, protecting them, inspiring them with its beauty, reminding them of the greater, infinite beauty of God Who created the heavens and the earth...

To me... the golden dome of St. Peter's was like God's own crown resting gloriously and majestically over some of his most precious possessions... the relics of His apostles, his Saints and popes, and, over that person He has chosen to guide His children to their eternal home... the Vicar of Christ himself...

Michelangelo was most certainly inspired when he created the dome for St. Peter's — and perhaps... I wondered... did *he* see something like a Crown of God in what he was building for the Honor and Glory of God...?

Our third day in Rome began again with Mass. This morning we went to Mass in Our Holy Father's own private chapel. This time, there wasn't such a feast of beauty and mammoth glory to distract us as there was in *St. Peter's.* We paid more attention to the Mass iteslf, and once again, thrilled to being present at a Mass celebrated *by the Supreme Pontiff himself.* We were never quite able to suppress the sensation of elation and excitement we felt at being present during a Pontifical Mass right in the very heart of the Eternal City ... a Mass being celebrated by the successor to the Prince of Apostles, the Chief Shepherd and Bishop of Rome ... *the Head of the Universal Church ...*

The Holy Father says Mass beautifully, gracefully, everything liturgically correct. We were able to follow the Mass easily in our missal ... and at this particular Mass, the *Te igitur* right after the Sanctus was especially interesting ...

"Therefore, most gracious Father, we humbly beg of Thee and entreat Thee, through Jesus Christ, Thy Son, our Lord, to deem acceptable and bless these gifts, these offerings, these holy and unspotted oblations, which we offer unto Thee in first instance for Thy holy and Catholic Church, that Thou wouldst deign to give her peace and protection, to unite and guide her the whole world over; together with THY servant ... PIUS ... our Pope ... !"

What a great privilege to be able to say that right here, with *"Pius, our Pope"* celebrating the Mass himself ...

How good God has been to the Church to give us as courageous and as good a Pope as this in an age that needs leadership and guidance such as he has been giving us ... I resolved to live a much better life than I had up to now ... to give better example to others, to be a Catholic in the fullest sense of the name ... not only on Sundays for an hour or so, but *every* day—and *twenty four hours a day ...*

No matter how busy his schedule is—and whose schedule could be busier or more hectic than his?—Our Holy Father always makes time to spend in prayer and meditation before the Blessed Sacrament. We happened to be kneeling in the back of the chapel when he came in, so we remained in silence there for a few moments before leaving...

I recalled that *Bishop Fulton Sheen* once mentioned that *he* spends an hour before the Blessed Sacrament each day—and the bishop must have quite a busy schedule himself. He frequently advises his listeners to spend some time alone with God each day...

Now here was the *Supreme Pontiff,* who probably had a thousand things he could do, things that were important, critical, serious; things that were just waiting for him... but obviously, the Vicar of Christ realizes that the outcome, the success of all his actions, and the ability to accomplish all these things comes from this place right here —the Tabernacle of the Most High... the Source of Life itself... the Fount of Wisdom and Knowledge and Grace ...the Miracle Worker of Galilee...the Divine Physician...

As we genuflected and slid quietly out, I resolved that I would never be *"too busy"* to stop in before the Blessed Sacrament and spend some time with the One Who *gives* me each new day, and thank Him for all His gifts and graces and blessings as well as for the trials and tribulations that He permits me to have—for my greater good...

If the *Holy Father* can find the time, I thought, I *certainly* ought to be able to...

Our priest-guide had arranged for a private audience for us. As we approached the room which Our Holy Father used for his office, we trembled with excitement... *imagine meeting the Vicar of Christ himself!* ... and actually talking with him! It was thrilling to contemplate.

As we entered the room, Our Holy Father was reading a large, thick book which had been sent to him for his birthday . . . When he saw us, he closed the book, and stood up to greet us. We knelt down and kissed his ring, one of the most magnificent rings we have ever seen! While we were trying to find the power to speak, His Holiness asked us how long we had been in Rome, what we had seen, how we had been enjoying ourselves and what we thought of various things . . . We answered mostly in brief sentences or in a few words. He realized our nervousness and continued speaking about *St.*

Peter's and *The Vatican* until we were more at ease... we were tremendously grateful for his thoughtfulness, and realized now how truly gracious he was...

He asked us then, where we came from, and then mentioned the name of our bishop whom he knew well... and other priests and monsignori of our diocese... he asked about our work, our families, our Catholic activities... and before we realized it, we were having an easy conversation with this great Pope!

Finally, our priest-guide asked the Supreme Pontiff if we might

have his special blessing. We knelt down and the Holy Father blessed each one of us individually. Then he gave us each a large medallion as a souvenir of our visit with him; we knelt, kissed his ring again, thanked him most warmly, and left with the feeling that we had just visited and spoken with Our Lord Himself. In a way, I suppose we had, for was not the Pope Christ's Vicar on earth, the visible head of His Church? . . .

This experience was most certainly the high point of our pilgrimage . . . and it will always remain an *unforgettable* experience . . .

After we left Our Holy Father's office in the Vatican Palace, we went downstairs, through the courtyard and out to St. Peter's Square. We were going to visit the Vatican Gardens because our guide thought it would help us to relax after the excitement and emotional drama of our visit with Pope Pius XII . . .

We paused near the statue of *St. Paul* in front of the great basilica, to examine the medallions Our Holy Father had given us. This particular one commemorated the tenth year of his pontificate. One side bore a superb likeness of the Pope — while the reverse side depicted him addressing a throng from the central balcony of St. Peter's.

Our priest-guide told us that tomorrow, just such an event was
scheduled to take place, so we would be able to see the real thing.
He was going to try to get us a place on the balcony, right behind
the Holy Father . . .

We started looking forward to it with great interest . . . meanwhile,
he led us past St. Peter's and the statue of *St. Peter* on the other side
of the basilica, through the arch under the bells on the left . . . passing
the statue of *Charlemagne* . . . then past the sacristy adjoining St.
Peter's . . . past the law court and jail *(we were surprised to see)* . . .
past the church of *St. Stephen, Martyr* . . . past the imposing *Governor's Palace* . . . and the *Ethiopian College* . . .

From this beautiful spot behind St. Peter's, we were able to see much of Vatican City all around us . . . and our guide told us that the Holy Father himself often walks here saying his office. At that time, no one is permitted in this area.

The tower on the right, our priest-guide told us, was one of the four Vatican Radio Towers. The *Vatican Radio Station* was inaugurated on February 12th, 1931 by Pope Pius XI at ceremonies attended by *Guglielmo Marconi,* the radio pioneer. Also present was the Pope's Secretary of State, *Eugene Cardinal Pacelli!*

At the time of its launching, Vatican Radio was the most powerful station in the world. It began with one 10-kilowatt transmitter but now has seven. It broadcasts ten hours daily in 29 languages to all parts of the world, even behind the Iron Curtain . . .

Inscribed on the ceiling of the Station's Chapel is its motto, taken from St. Matthew: *"Preach from the roof-tops."* Vatican Radio's call letters are *HVJ* and it has a studio right in St. Peter's Basilica! *HVJ* recently celebrated its 25th anniversary! . . .

This was an interesting contrast to many of the ancient things we had seen — and merely proved to us that the Church was as modern as the age in which it lived . . . it uses the things of the world, for the good of the world, for the good of the people . . . always striving to bring them closer to God, and God closer to the people . . .

Almost directly behind St. Peter's, at the foot of the basilica—not far from the walls of Vatican city—we came to this beautiful tiny railroad station. Made of marble, it is in keeping with the other buildings of Vatican City and gives direct railroad facilities to the world outside.

However, our guide told us, it is rarely used now for passenger traffic, but is strictly a freight depot where goods are brought in to Vatican City free of Italian customs duty.

Long ago, when the papal state consisted of a large part of

central Italy, we were told, the railroad station was then also used for passengers. Pope Pius IX had his coach of state here, and later on we saw it in a Roman museum. It is called *"the little train of Pius IX"* —*il trenino di Pio IX* ...

In fact, our priest-guide told us, the Vatican once had its own merchant fleet at *Civitavecchia,* northwest of Rome, which was its own harbor! According to a clause in the Lateran Treaty, the Papacy *still* has a right to these things, but up to now, has chosen not to avail itself of its own harbor or a fleet of ships!

While strolling through the Vatican grounds, we came across one of the *Palatine Guards*. They were established, our guide informed us, in 1850 by *Pope Pius IX*. They are also known as the *Guardia d'Onore*. Membership is restricted to Roman citizens because they are used to defend their own bishop, the Pope, who is the Bishop of Rome.

There are now some 500 members of the *Palatine Guard,* who serve without pay and whose backgrounds vary from university professors to manual laborers. This particular guard told us that he used to be a bank clerk, and likes this much more than what he was doing before ... he considers it a great privilege to serve the Bishop of Rome ... to be one of the *Guardia d'Onore* ... because they guard the person of the Holy Father, his living quarters, and attend him at all public functions as well as in the papal chapels ...

It was interesting to talk to him.

One of the buildings we stopped in to see was the *Pontifical Candle Factory.* This is where they make all the candles used for the many and various ceremonies in St. Peter's and The Vatican chapels. Forty workers at this candle factory, they told us, turn out an average of 7,500 candles every day!

They also paint these candles for Holy Years and for Easter, the paschal candles. This man told us that it usually takes an entire day to paint a candle this size . . .

The array of candles was most colorful and every detail was clearly painted . . . each one of these candles was a work of art . . . !

After leaving here, we passed a place that displayed the papal robes. Our priest-guide explained the various items and told us when the pope would wear each one. The striking feature in the window was the red velvet cape with the ermine border . . . called a *mozzetta.* And the red hat below it . . .

Passing the *Sacristy,* our priest guide led us inside to take a look at the vestments, chalices and other sacred vessels used during the Mass and the many other ceremonies performed in the vast basilica.

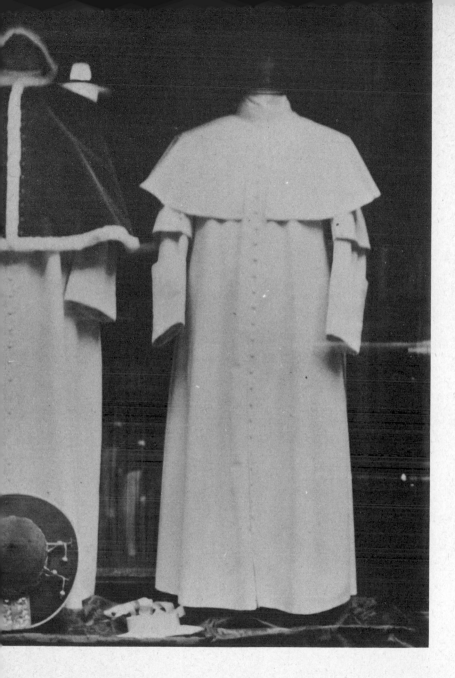

One of the brothers, a member of the *Vatican ceremonial staff*, showed us the magnificent golden vestments; and the vestments used for various Masses, red, green, white, purple, black and rose...the chalices adorned with gems and exquisite carvings were *out of this world!*

Finally, he showed us the papal *tiara* and *mitre*. He explained that the tiara is worn by the Holy Father only at his coronation and on other occasions afterward that are not liturgical. When pontificating at liturgical ceremonies, such as the Mass, etc., he wears a mitre like any other bishop.

The origin of the tiara we were told, is uncertain and the significance of the three crowns has various interpretations. Some say it is a symbol of the Church Militant, Suffering and Triumphant; or of the spiritual powers of teaching, ruling and sanctifying. Some maintain it symbolizes the Trinity, Father, Son and Holy Spirit.

The tiara is placed upon the newly elected pope's head with these words:

Receive this tiara adorned with three crowns and know that you are the father of princes and of kings; guide of the world; and vicar upon earth of Christ Jesus our Savior.

The close look we got of the tiara showed it to be made of elegant silver cloth and the three crowns adorned with many beautiful jewels, rubies, sapphires, diamonds, pearls, amethysts and emeralds. It was absolutely magnificent!

Our priest-guide, who was a scripture scholar, explained that a tiara or mitre was first worn by *Aaron,* the first high priest, brother of *Moses,* and his successors in the ancient Hebrew priesthood.

If you look through the Bible in *Exodus* (29:6-9 and 39:26, 30) he told us, you'll find reference to the first tiara or mitre. It was higher than that worn by the priests and from it hung a purple ribbon to which a golden plate was attached. On the plate were engraved the words: "*Sacred to the Lord*"—a reference to this will also be found in *Ecclesiasticus* 45:14.

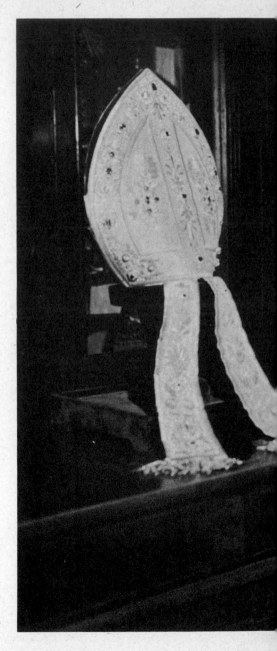

The papal mitre was also adorned with jewels, but not as many as the triple-crowned tiara. In the consecration of a bishop, our guide told us, the mitre is symbolically considered as the *helmet of salvation* ...

Following this, we were shown some hats worn by cardinals...

These are the kinds of hats which will be worn by each of the prelates elevated to the Sacred College of Cardinals at the consistory. The center one on top is the famous *"red hat"* or *galero,* symbol of the cardinal's office. It was a brilliant red felt and from its broad brim usually hang 15 tassels.

The red hat is worn by a cardinal only once, then set aside until his death, when it is placed on his catafalque, then suspended from the roof of his cathedral directly over the crypt where he lies buried.

I remember seeing three red hats suspended from the top of *St. Patrick's Cathedral* in New York.

On the left is the black ceremonial hat with gold embroidery and on the right the hat normally worn by a cardinal, black felt with a cordon of gold.

Below these are the scarlet *biretta* of moire silk and the *zucchetto*, or skull cap, also made of moire silk. It certainly was a very colorful display ...

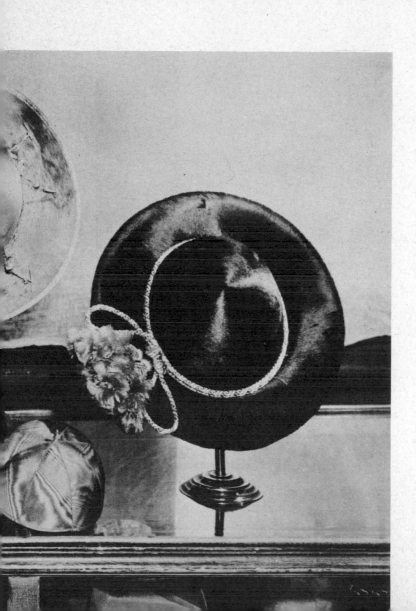

As long as we were talking about cardinals, our priest-guide wanted us to see the room where a cardinal stayed during the conclave for the election of a new pope.

As we made our way through St. Peter's to the *Vatican Palace*, we had visions of a glorious apartment with magnificent fittings, drapes, tapestries, thick Oriental rugs, and furniture that would be in keeping with a cardinal's exalted position as a prince of the Church.

I could hardly believe my eyes! *THIS was a cardinal's bedroom...?* It was almost as plain and as simple as the cell of a Trappist monk! We were told that this room becomes the only living quarters of a cardinal all during the election. The contrast from what we expected to see almost made us gasp in astonishment. But the Holy Father encourages simplicity and despite the fact that he is

the Pope, despite the fact that the Vatican Palace has so many art treasures of various kinds, the papal living quarters are *also* quite unpretentious and marvelous examples of stark simplicity!

I suppose that after all the magnificence and color and beauty of the pontifical ceremonies, it might almost be a relief to return to something as plain and ordinary as this cardinal's bedroom.

In two hours from now, the Holy Father was going to give the red hat to a newly created cardinal, and our guide had tickets for us to attend the ceremony. We made our way to St. Peter's where this was to take place, so that we would be sure to have good seats near the papal throne... which was to be set up, we were told, right in front of the *Altar of Confession*...

The ceremony of a newly-created cardinal receiving his red hat is truly impressive. We were fortunate in being able to watch it from a front row! The cardinals knelt before the Holy Father while two other cardinals held the red hat over the newly initiated. *"Receive this red hat,"* declared the Pope at this moment, *"as a special badge of the cardinal's rank. By this you are to understand that you must show yourself fearless even to the shedding of your blood in making our holy Faith respected, in securing peace for Christian people and in promoting the welfare of the Holy Catholic Church..."*

The rich colors of the tapestry behind the throne, and the shimmering scarlet moire of many cardinals' robes made this a most colorful ceremony . . .

Afterwards, we kissed the rings of the new cardinals and offered our sincere congratulations . . . who knows . . . maybe one of these cardinals will be the next pope . . . ? At least, they will bear the responsibility of choosing the successor to *Pius XII.*

It's really wonderful how the Church carries on, from age to age, from pope to pope . . . creating new cardinals . . . consecrating new bishops . . . ordaining new priests . . . dispensing the sacraments to men, women and children all over the world . . . jealously guarding the sanctity of marriage . . . blessing new brides and grooms . . . baptizing their children . . . teaching them . . . guiding them . . . preparing them for battle with the world, the flesh and the devil . . . watching them enter seminaries, monasteries, convents . . . getting married . . . raising families . . . ordaining new priests . . . dispensing the sacraments . . . consecrating new bishops . . . creating new cardinals . . . electing new popes.

It's really wonderful how the Church carries on . . . from age to age, from pope to pope . . . creating new cardinals . . .

After the new members of the Sacred College of Cardinals were given their red hats...the Holy Father read the final benediction from this elaborately-bound liturgical book.

After it was all over, our priest guide took us into the sacristy again where *Brother Frederico,* another member of the Vatican ceremonial staff, showed us the book at close range. The illuminations, the golds, reds and blues, the beautiful hand printed lettering and the decorative designs made this a real work of art. He also showed us a few of the altar-missals used during the Masses in St. Peter's, and the special missal used by Our Holy Father. *It was absolutely magnificent!*

This led to a discussion of the *Vatican Library.*

And Brother Frederico was just the one to give us the facts. Pope *Nicholas* V was instrumental in beginning the Vatican Library, he told us, around the 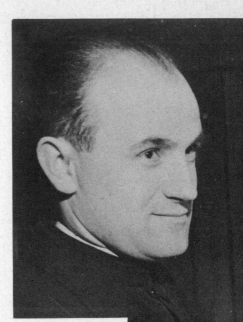 year 1450. He even had a printing press installed in the library building at the Vatican after Gutenberg invented it and the pope realized its tremendous possibilities.

Pope *Sixtus IV* engaged scholars to care for the books which grew to number 3,500. *Leo X* wanted to make Rome the center of learning. *Sixtus V* had his architect build the *Sixtine Library,* a separate building for housing the Vatican library. Almost every later pope added in some way to the expansion or improvement of the library. Famous private collections were either donated or bought...some containing priceless manuscripts.

When *Leo XIII* became pope, the library had 60,000 manuscripts and about 500,000 books. But practically none of these were catalogued! Under the direction of the great Pope Leo, the formidable job of making order out of chaos was begun. The Vatican Library was completely organized and orderly and opened to all true scholars of any religion or creed, or of none. *"We have nothing to fear from the truth"* he said.

Each Pope wills the *Vatican Library* to his successor, according to custom. *Pius XI* was a great book lover and realizing the great value of the many thousands of books already contained in the *Vatican Library,* and watching a veritable avalanche of books constantly being donated to the library, he decided that modern methods would be needed to cope with the situation!

The *Morgan Foundation* offered to help finance the re-establishment of a working library at the Vatican. The pontiff accepted the offer, and himself supervised the work. One of the scholars assisting him was *Nicholas Murray Butler.* An American library designer was engaged to install new American equipment. More than seven miles of steel shelving was constructed to support the tremendous amount and weight of the books—over 500,000 volumes!

One of the interesting features of the library that we saw, was the *Laboratorio Vaticano*—a book hospital which uses new and almost miraculous methods of repairing seemingly hopelessly damaged books. This was under the direction of *Cardinal Tisserant,* who had arranged this pilgrimage for us; and who takes a lively interest in the upkeep and efficiency of the *Vatican Library.*

Some of the interesting things we saw were the letters of *King Henry VIII* to *Anne Boleyn;* the breviary of *St. Gregory;* one of the earliest Chinese books in existence on paper that was incredibly thin! And many, many others . . . including the original writings of many of the Saints, and Popes. We even saw some of the *Dead Sea Scrolls* being processed . . .

After we left, passing through one of the offices used by Vatican personnel, we came across this priest apparently punching a time card! We were introduced to *Father Luigi Panaioli* who was punching out at the end of his morning shift! He noticed our astonishment and explained . . .

This was one of 40 time clocks set up in Vatican offices for the first time in history. The purpose of the new time-control plan, he explained was to end late arrivals and early departures by staff members of Vatican bureaus and to regulate absences. This is part of the modernizing process, he said, which almost every section of the Vatican is undergoing.

"How about Cardinals," we asked. *"Do they have to punch in and out too?"*

Father Luigi smiled. *"The only ones exempt from this system,"* he said, *"are their Eminences, the Cardinal Secretaries of Congregations, the Episcopal heads of other offices—and —the Swiss Guards."* We thanked him for this interesting information and took our leave. He might only have an hour for lunch, we thought, so we didn't want to take up any more of his time . . .

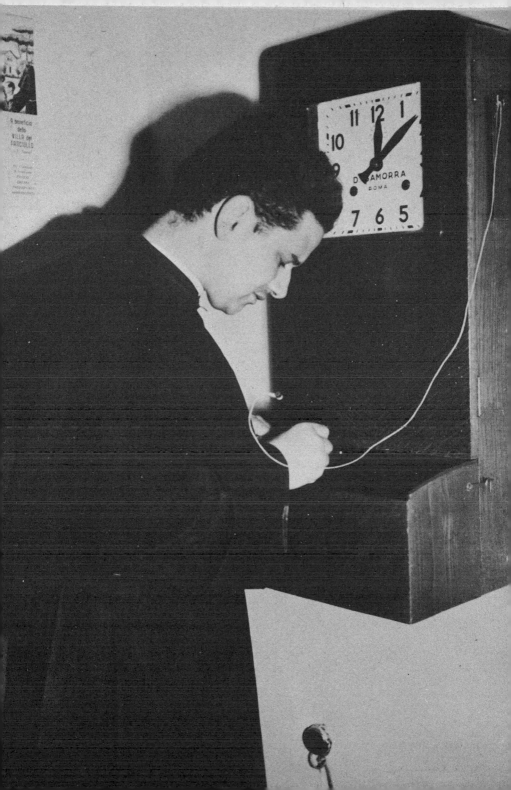

On the way out, we came to this area that looked like it might be the Sistine Chapel's refuse collecting depot. We couldn't quite figure it out until our priest-guide explained that this insignificant looking corner was a very important place at certain times...for instance, the time between the death of one pope and the election of a new one.

This small silver stove with its long, white pipe is the only means by which the outside world first learns that a new pope has been elected. After each vote is taken, the ballots are burned here in this stove. When no candidate has yet been elected, straw is mixed with the ballots. This causes thick black smoke to rise above the outside of the chapel.

When the new pope is finally chosen, white smoke comes from the chimney outside giving the happy news to the waiting crowds in St. Peter's Square...

To give us some idea how this would look, our priest guide took some of the straw and papers in one of the baskets near the stove, and put them inside the stove. *Of course*, he told us, *this is strictly not permitted, but since there is no papal election at this time, and no crowds watching outside, no one will really mind. They'll just think some rubbish is being burned*...I gave father my cigarette lighter and he ignited the paper.

We hurried outside to see what the smoke at a papal election looks like...

Outside, in *St. Peter's Square*, we looked up toward the *Sistine Chapel* and right in front of it was the top part of our long white stovepipe, sending up a few wispy puffs of black smoke from the little pile of paper and straw that father had ignited a few moments before. This black smoke would indicate that a new pope had not yet been chosen — that the votes resulted in a stalemate — up to this point.

It was interesting to see inasmuch as the possibility of our being here during a papal election ... was fairly remote. We got a preview of it anyway. No one else in the great square even noticed the smoke ...

While we stood there looking up at the *Sistine Chapel* behind our little smokestack, our priest guide pointed to the building at the right, with the shuttered windows. That was the *Vatican Palace* — and these windows belonged to the papal apartments ... or were very close to them ...

The *Vatican Palace*, we were informed, is the largest in the world. They don't know the exact number of rooms it contains, but it is over 1,000! By far the greatest number of these are occupied by collections, show-rooms, chapels, salons and private apartments. A comparatively small part of the building is set apart for the Holy Father's personal use.

The Vatican did not become the usual residence of the popes until after their return from *Avignon*, when the Lateran was deserted. After the death of *Gregory XI*, the first conclave was held in the Vatican in 1378. In 1450, *Nicholas V*, who wanted to make the Vatican the most imposing palace in the world, determined to unite all the government offices and the residences of the cardinals in this one palace. The small portion completed by him and later occupied by *Alexander VI* and named *Tor di Borgia*, was extended by subsequent popes. In 1473 the *Sistine Chapel* was erected by *Sixtus IV*, from whom it gets its name.

Urban VIII erected the *Scala Regia* from Bernini's design; *Pius VII*, the *Braccio Nuovo* for the sculptures; *Gregory XVI*, the *Etruscan Museum* and *Pius IX* closed the court side of the *Cortile di S. Damaso* by covering and reconstructing the great staircase which leads from the arcades of the piazza into the court. The palace now has about 20 courts ...

Looking up, we also got a good close view of the statues on the colonnades. Each of them is 18 feet tall! And these were only a few of the 164 standing around *St. Peter's Square* ...

Since we were talking about papal elections, our priest-guide thought we might like to see some of the equipment used by the cardinals during an election for a new pope. He took us to a room adjoining the *Sistine Chapel* where the election takes place, and here we saw what looked like a huge ciborium and a huge chalice, plus another odd, oriental-looking bowl. In front of these were a lot of little balls that looked like ping-pong balls.

These are used to determine the order in which the cardinals place their ballots in the chalice on the altar of the Sistine Chapel.

A man who was a member of the *Vatican Staff* explained the entire procedure to us. The election held to choose a new pope is called a *Conclave,* which means: a meeting that takes place in a room closed *cum clave,* with a key. When the cardinals assemble for a *Conclave,* they are actually under lock and key until a new Pope is elected!

If a new Pope is not elected within the first three days, the Cardinals' meals are reduced to a single dish of food in the morning and another at night. After five days, if they still have not decided, they only get bread and water! This is because in the year 1271, when 18 Cardinals came together to elect a successor to *Pope Clement IV,* they were still undecided after eighteen months! The roof of the hall where the Cardinals met was removed, every door was locked and all supplies were cut off! In a few days, the tired and hungry Cardinals elected a new pope who took the name of *Gregory X.*

Inspired by this efficient election, the new Pope summoned a Council and a *Brief* was issued which fixed the new procedure for papal elections. Those rules drawn up in July 1274 still apply today, and keeping the Cardinals under lock and key is one of them ...

We were invited to take a really close look at these golden vessels used by the Cardinals during the elections. This is the great chalice used as a ballot box for the voting papers of the College of Cardinals during the *Conclave*. It is placed on the altar in the *Sistine Chapel* where the voting takes place. The Vatican Staff man showed us one of the ballots used by the Cardinals at this time and how it is placed into a slot in a cover of the chalice...

This method of secret voting, he told us, comprises three operations: the ante-writing, the writing and the telling.

For the ante-writing the ballot papers have to be prepared, then the name a particular cardinal wants is written on his ballot, after which it is folded in a special way, sealed, and then extracted...five operations all together.

Counting the votes consists of eight operations: handing over the papers by each Cardinal; swearing before the Altar according to the prescribed formula; placing the paper into the great chalice here shown, which is on the Altar; mixing of the papers and counting the votes by the tellers; publishing of the results by the three tellers, the third reading aloud of the name so that each Cardinal can record upon a special paper, the development of the election; clipping the papers together and finally putting them into the other chalice which has been placed upon a table.

Following this, the tellers count the votes, and after noting the count, they burn the papers in the little stove we saw before, assisted by the *Pontifical Masters of Ceremonies*...

All in all, a very complicated, but necessary procedure...

Not being cardinals, there would be no opportunity of seeing these things during an election, so we were grateful to the Vatican Staff man for letting us see them now, and for explaining the procedure to us...

Our priest-guide then took us to another interesting place in The Vatican—*The Vatican Pharmacy*—or, drug store. All the residents of Vatican City including the Holy Father and the entire Papal Court, get their prescriptions filled here. The Vatican Pharmacy is operated by the *Brothers of Charity*, who are experts in the pharmaceutical field.

It reminded me of the *Alexian Brothers* who are all registered nurses and staff their own hospitals; of the *Nursing Sisters of the*

Sick Poor, all of whom are also registered nurses; of *Mother Anna Dengel's Medical Mission Sisters,* many of whom are real doctors and go to India to help the poor women there who are not permitted to see male doctors...and lots of other Religious Orders where the Sisters and Brothers are professional members of the medical profession.

And so here, the good brother showed us around, pointing out to us how prescriptions are filled, how the drugs are kept, explaining

what various drugs might be used for, etc., he demonstrated by his knowledge that he was a true pharmacist! Strict records are kept of everything, and only the best ingredients will be used in filling prescriptions. He told us that the Brothers also run a *First Aid Station* when large crowds gather, and in fact they were just beginning to set one up now in St. Peter's for the beatification ceremony that was scheduled there this afternoon.

At the mention of the beatification ceremony, our priest-guide remembered that we had better start getting over there. He had tickets for us in one of the balconies near the *Confession Altar* that will give us some excellent views of the entire ceremony. We thanked the Brother for his kindness and bid him *"buona sera..."*

Upon leaving the pharmacy, we couldn't help noting how different it was from our downtown drug stores back home which seemed like gaudy miniature imitations of a five-and-ten...and where sometimes, one has to ask a clerk where *the drug counter is...!*

St. Peter's was already quite full of people; many members of Religious Orders in their varied and colorful habits; Noble Guards, Swiss Guards and other members of the Vatican ceremonial staff...

Our guide took us quickly through the vast basilica toward the great statue of *St. Longinus* in a niche in one of the four tremendous piers that support the great dome. We went through an arched doorway, up some stairs and came out on a balcony overlooking the beautiful *Altar of Confession.* The balcony was at an angle facing the rear of the basilica which is called, father told us, the *apse.*

From here we got a remarkably excellent view of the *Altar of the Chair,* another of the great masterpieces of *Giovanni Lorenzo Bernini.* Here, gigantic statues of four doctors of the Church, *Sts. Augustine and Ambrose* and *Sts. Athanasius and John Chrysostom* triumphantly support a graceful bronze throne (or *cathedra*) containing the wooden chair inlaid with ivory which tradition maintains was presented to St. Peter by *Senator Pudens* and used by the first pope when preaching. A magnificent window supported by graceful angels shows the Holy Spirit in the form of a dove in a glory of light. The entire altarpiece is majestic and tremendously impressive.

Now the ceremony has begun... 3,000 *Brothers of the Christian Schools,* as well as many of their friends and other guests, are here to witness this solemn ceremony beatifying *Brother Benildus,* a French-born member of the Order who died in 1862. A tapestry showing a scene in his life is at the right just opposite us...

Our Holy Father kneels before the magnificent altar, flanked by cardinals, archbishops, bishops and the colorfully garbed Papal Guards... The lights and the color and the beauty of St. Peter's... the chanting of the choir ... and everything about this beatification made us think we were getting a peek into Heaven...! It was just too glorious to behold... we thought, as we watched, enchanted and thrilled beyond words... *what must heaven really be like...?*

After the beatification ceremony for *Brother Benildus* was over, our priest-guide led us down from the balcony and over to one of the thrones used by Our Holy Father. He wanted us to get a close look at it...

The carving was intricate and masterful...the papal emblems of the tiara and the keys on top were done in exquisite detail.

The colorful tapestry on the back of the throne showed Our Lord giving the keys to St. Peter and under them the words:

TU ES PETRUS...*Thou art Peter*...

This was a massive chair! It was constructed in 1819 for *Pope Pius VII* and made of gilded wood. The right arm bears the date: 1819, while the left arm is dated 1827...The Holy Father uses this throne when he formally announces the creation of new cardinals at a *Vatican Consistory*, and also on other important occasions.

Our priest-guide searched in his wallet and drew out a snapshot he had which happened to show the Pontiff on this very throne, when he was addressing an important gathering of the *College of Cardinals*...not so long ago...

TV ES PETRVS

Our guide next led us to the *Clementine Hall* in the Vatican Palace where Our Holy Father was to receive a few hundred American pilgrims. They had been to an *International Eucharistic Congress* and after visits to *Fatima* and *Lourdes,* wanted to see the Vicar of Christ before going back home...

We went through the Bronze Door at the end of the right-hand colonnade, past the Swiss Guards and up the *staircase of Pius IX* ... past the offices of the *Maestro di Camera* on the first floor, continued up the stairs

and came out in the *Cortile di San Damaso* which was, as usual, guarded by the papal gendarmes. We noticed the time on the clock on the north side. We passed the fountain erected by *Pope St. Damasus,* after whom the court is named ... On the right, under a porch, we saw the entrance to the papal apartments.

The *Scalone Nobile,* up which the pilgrims go, is dominated by large, modern stained glass windows showing Sts. Peter and Paul. On the first floor, we passed a Swiss Guard on duty before the apartment of the Secretary of State. After climbing two more flights we reached the *Sala Clementina,* where the Holy Father was already greeting the pilgrims. There were many bishops, monsignori and even a cardinal, we noticed. These dignitaries in their colorful red and purple robes, remained with their own groups and went with the Holy Father from pilgrim to pilgrim, sometimes whispering something to the Supreme Pontiff about a particular person ...

When they were all finished, the photographers wanted to take some pictures of the Holy Father with the bishops, monsignori, and cardinals. The photographers took a position right next to where we stood, so we got an excellent view of all these princes of the church ... His Eminence, *Francis Cardinal Spellman* of New York stood to the Holy Father's right, while *Archbishop John O'Hara* of Philadelphia stood at the Pontiff's left ...

Our priest guide next took us to the balcony of *St. Peter's Basilica* where the Holy Father was to address some 80,000 athletes who had come to Rome on the 10th anniversary of their *Catholic Sports Center*. We followed the Supreme Pontiff after he had finished the picture taking in *Clementine Hall,* and were able to stand almost directly behind him as he addressed these young athletes. There were tremendous cheers upon his arrival . . .

The Pope spoke for almost half an hour on ethics in sports and its natu-

ral Christian virtues... When the Holy Father was finished speaking, these athletes put on a real spectacle for him. They did calisthenics... juggling ... acrobatics... and they even gave a short basketball exhibition which His Holiness enjoyed tremendously.

We also got an excellent view of Rome and looked straight down the Via Conciliazione to the Castel Sant'Angelo to the left of the Obelisk... The entire scene brought a strong reminder of the back of the medal which the Holy Father had given us a few days ago...

Right in the midst of our pilgrimage, we attended a concert at the Vatican Palace! The Holy Father's secretary had sent word to us to be sure we joined His Holiness this afternoon for a concert to be given by the Israel Philharmonic Orchestra.

"The Israel Philharmonic Orchestra?!?" we asked, puzzled. Yes, our guide assured us, they were giving this private concert for the Pope in gratitude for the extensive help which he and the Catholic Church had

given to numerous Jewish people, and others, persecuted by Hitler and Mussolini, during World War II. All the Jewish men, women and children who sought sanctuary in the Vatican were sheltered here under direct orders from Pope Pius XII and given every possible assistance. The Holy Father's influence was used in a thousand different ways to protect, safeguard and care for Jewish refugees, not only in the Vatican, but all over Europe during the war. Catholic monasteries and convents gave shelter to as many as it was physically possible for them to help...

In 1945, our guide informed us, *The Hadassah Society of America* sent $10,000 to the Holy Father in grateful recognition of his charity to the Jews of Europe all during the frightful war years ... *The Vatican Information Office* united many Jewish and other families who had become separated or lost during the war.

So now, the *Israel Philharmonic Orchestra* had come to the Vatican to show their gratitude to this beloved and humanitarian Pontiff, for his paternal assistance to the Jewish people. They played some favorites of the Holy Father from Beethoven and Bach, and some beautiful compositions of Richard Wagner to whose music the Pontiff is rather partial. He especially enjoyed Wagner's *"Forest Murmurs"* and the excerpts from *"Lohengrin."*

This was the first time that any orchestra from outside Italy had played privately for His Holiness, who posed afterward, for a photograph with the orchestra. Conductor *Paul Kletzky* stood at the Holy Father's left. I shall always remember this remarkable concert—*in the Vatican!...*

After the concert, we accompanied the Supreme Pontiff to the *Astrophysics Laboratory*. This was an extension of the *Pontifical Observatory* which was first built under Pope Gregory's direction when he instituted the calendar reform.

The object of this laboratory, which is operated by the Jesuits, is to explain the results which have been obtained with the telescope and astrograph by spectral-analytical work.

Astrophysics, our guide explained, is the science that deals principally with the constitution of heavenly, or celestial bodies — he name comes from a combination of the words *astronomy* and *physics.* Astronomy was only a study of the movement and position of stars, planets, galaxies, etc. Astrophysics is also a record of their composition and quality. And an astrograph, he told us, is a photographic telescope.

The Holy Father was greeted by *Father Louis Gatterer* of the Lab Staff, who introduced the other members of the staff to His Holiness. Father Gatterer explained the operation of the spectrograph to the Pontiff, who showed a keen interest in the work of this laboratory. Astronomical discoveries made by this lab have contributed important information and findings to science.

It was an interesting visit, and even *more* interesting, was the Holy Father's universal quest for knowledge in so many varied fields ... One usually thinks of the Supreme Pontiff as being interested in purely spiritual or pious affairs. But his interest extends to every sphere of activity which occupies the mind and the heart of man ... *even,* we found, *astrophysics!*

The Holy Father's Secretary reminded him that it was getting near the time for the *Corpus Christi* procession which was to take place in St. Peter's Square soon...so after a few more words with *Father Gatterer* and the other men on the Lab Staff, and commending them for their excellent work, the Supreme Pontiff left for the Sacristy adjoining the great basilica...

As we made our own way to *St. Peter's Square* shortly after the Holy Father left, our priest-guide explained something to us about an interesting part of the *Corpus Christi* procession which we were going to witness... It seems that in the year 1264, in a little church not far from Rome, a priest was saying Mass. He was experiencing great difficulty believing the mystery of transubstantiation...and in fact, so the story goes, actually began to doubt the Real Presence of Christ in the consecrated Host. So at this Mass, right after he pronounced the words of consecration:

HOC EST ENIM CORPUS MEUM...

the Sacred Host suddenly and miraculously began to bleed! Word of this startling miracle reached the ears of *Pope Urban IV* who was just then considering whether or not to extend the *Feast of Corpus Christi* to the entire Church. The miracle was evidently authenticated, enough to persuade *Pope Urban* to definitely extend the feast without any hesitation, to the whole Church...

This Host was contained in a 200-pound silver reliquary, richly decorated with precious jewels, which was brought down from *Orvieto,* in Umbria, about 60 miles north of Rome, for the first time. The centuries-old reliquary was to be carried in the procession by students of the *German-Hungarian Pontifical College...*

We finally got to St. Peter's Square, and watched the procession come out of St. Peter's Basilica. The students carrying the reliquary with the miraculous Host led the procession... Our Holy Father kneeling before a small portable altar, followed. His lips moved silently as he prayed before the Blessed Sacrament in the golden monstrance before him...

A beautiful white and gold silk canopy was carried over the Blessed Sacrament and Our Holy Father. The traditional *Flabellum,* the fans used at important pontifical functions, were on either side of the Supreme Pontiff. These decorative fans of graceful plumes were used many centuries ago to keep insects from the Sacred Host and from the priest during Mass, especially in hot climates. But now they are used as a mark of honor for bishops, princes and other royal dignitaries. Two are always used at the Vatican whenever the Pope is carried in state on the *sedia gestatoria* to or from the altar or audience chambers...

The procession went all around the square, around the Obelisk and back into St. Peter's on the other side... All the while, I thought *...here was Christ himself, with the Vicar of Christ...together...how many things They had to talk about...how many people They blessed as They passed through our midst ...thousands and thousands of people gathered to pay homage to the Prince of Peace and to the Pope of Peace...what a wonderful sight to behold...what a wonderful privilege to have the Faith that we have ...and the great heritage of twenty centuries ...Tu es Petrus..."and upon this Rock I will build My Church..."*

After the *Corpus Christi* procession...when the Sacred Host was returned to the tabernacle in the beautiful Blessed Sacrament altar in the basilica...preparations were made for a solemn canonization ceremony.

The foundress of the *Daughters of Our Lady of Mercy*, St. Maria Giuseppa Rossello, who died in 1880—*eight years before Don Bosco was to be canonized* in solemn ceremony this afternoon. It was a long ceremony, but a very impressive one, and surely one that brought great joy to the members of the *Daughters of Our Lady of Mercy*.

Our Holy Father, still flanked by the graceful white plumes of

the *flabellum,* stood up on the *sedia gestatoria* to give his papal blessing to the people. Because of the solemnity of a canonization, I noticed that he wore the *tiara* which we had gotten such a beautifully close look at before.

The energy of the Holy Father, and his stamina, were inexhaustible! We certainly were fortunate...we Catholics...and the Church ...yes! *and the world too!*...to have as good and as Christlike and as wonderful a pope like Pius XII...if only the world would listen to him...*if only the leaders of the countries of the world would listen to him*...then there would be peace in the world...and it would be *lasting* peace...if *only* they would listen to him.

On our way out of the basilica after the ceremonies, we passed the *Papal Flag,* and our priest guide asked if any of us knew the significance or the history of this flag. We all shook our heads sadly. None of us knew very much at all about it, except that there *was* such a flag. *"Won't you tell us what its history is, Father?"* I asked...

"Well, the yellow and white of the flag," he began, "were derived from the colors of the banner of *Godfrey de Bouillon* of Jerusalem who lived around the year 1100. These two colors are supposed to have originated from the usual gold and silver tinctures of the keys of St. Peter. Gold and yellow, and silver and white are interchangeable colors in heraldry," he explained.

"Godfrey, who was the *Duke of Lower Lorraine,* was called *'Defender of the Holy Sepulchre.'* He took part in the Crusades and in July 1099, with his brother Eustace, was the first to enter Jerusalem. He accepted the sovereignty of Jerusalem but refused to bear the title of king. Having received investiture from the patriarch, he defeated the Saracens in Egypt but died shortly thereafter. His tomb in the *Church of the Holy Sepulchre* in Jerusalem was destroyed in 1808.

"Now, the flag of the Vatican State is historically the same as the one adopted in the fifteenth century when the tiara and keys constituted the arms of the Pope, the church and its possessions. This blazon is: *a red cord, a pair of keys crossed, one gold, the other silver, surmounted by a tiara, silver crowned gold.*

"After the sixteenth century a different blazon was used for the temporary possessions of the Church, the crossed keys surmounted by the ombrellino. However, the new Vatican State under *Pope Pius XI* has used the insignia of the *spiritual* dominion of the Church, the keys and tiara, and also uses the white and gold field as used by *Godfrey de Bouillion* and the Kingdom of Jerusalem.

"One key," Father explained, "represents the power to bind and the other, the power to loose, as given to St. Peter by Christ. The triple crown, or tiara, which we saw the Holy Father wearing a little while ago, marks the pope as *the father of princes and of kings, guide of the world, and vicar upon earth of Christ, the Messiah.*

"That's about all there is to it," Father concluded, "except that, as you probably noticed in your parish church back home, the papal flag is usually on the epistle side in the sanctuary while the national flag is on the gospel side. If you have ever seen it in a parade or a procession, you probably noticed that the papal flag is carried on the left side of the national flag...

"And now I think, since it is so late, we had better be getting back to our hotel... don't you think?... remember, we have another big day ahead of us tomorrow..."

We thanked Father very much, and realized how much of a scholar and a historian he really was!

Tomorrow *was* to be another big day, and we had a date for early Mass in St. Peter's... a very unusual Mass this time...

We met our priest guide very early this morning at the Pieta, according to the arrangements we made last night. He took us past the Altar of Confession toward the Altar of the Chair in the apse, then through some doorways and up endless sections of spiral stairs. We seemed to be climbing to the top of the basilica and had to stop to rest every once in awhile. *Where in heaven was he taking us...?* Finally, when we came out, I thought that we *were* in Heaven! We were just under the roof of the apse at the back of the basilica! *What a view...!!!* Father certainly knew his way around!

When the ceremonies began, we got a bird's-eye view, or in this case, an *angel's*-eye view, of the ceremony below. The Holy Father was on the throne at the left, while *Patriarch Maximos IV* of the Melkite Rite celebrated a Pontifical Mass, our priest guide told us, at the specific request of the Holy Father. This Mass, at which representatives of almost all the Eastern Rites of the Church were present, was the *Byzantine Liturgy of St. John Chrysostum.* A temporary altar was set up for it right near the main altar, behind which we could see the marble stairs going down to the Crypt and St. Peter's tomb.

The concelebrants of the Liturgy, father informed us, included 14 bishops, 4 archimandrites and a canon belonging to various Oriental rites. I remembered a little Byzantine chapel back home where I occasionally attended the Liturgy, as they call the Mass, according to the rite of *St. John Chrysostum.* It is unlike the Latin Mass as we know it, except for the essentials, the consecration and Communion. An interesting thing about Communion here is that we receive under both species... The priest stands in one place while those who want to receive go up to him. He takes a cube of the Host which has been dipped into the chalice containing the Precious Blood, and with a tiny golden spoon, places It *inside* your mouth...

Here, I noticed only four ikons before the altar, whereas in the true Byzantine church, the walls are almost covered with ikons, many of which remind you of the famous picture of *Our Lady of Perpetual Help.* And in the Byzantine church, you can't see the altar which is behind some curtains, but here, out of necessity, the altar was exposed to open view. It was certainly interesting, and I found again that my Daily Missal was of absolutely no value to me during an Eastern Rite Mass, or Liturgy!

But the choir, without organ accompaniment, chanting hymns in Russian during the Liturgy, was absolutely superb! If I had not been to an Eastern Rite Mass before, I would almost think that I had not attended Mass! But it IS the Mass, just as surely and as truly as the Latin Rite is.

Perhaps, if we really understood it, we might think it was more beautiful than the Latin Rite...but — the Mass is the Mass, and it is beautiful in *any* rite...or... *in any language*...

Later that morning, our good friend, Cardinal Tisserant, invited us to meet some members of the Sacred Congregation of Rites. They were meeting in the Throne Room of the Apostolic Palace to discuss the martyrdom of 56 victims of the Chinese Boxer Rebellion in June 1900, and the heroic virtue of two nuns.

Nervous and awed by the thought of a roomful of cardinals, our priest-guide led us to the Throne Room and with the approval of two Swiss Guards, we entered. Our Holy Father stood in front of the papal throne. We were introduced once again to His Holiness by Cardinal Tisserant who stood at the Holy Father's right, and as we knelt to kiss the papal ring, The Supreme Pontiff told Cardinal Tisserant that we had already gotten to know one another, and that he hoped our pilgrimage in the Holy City was proving interesting

as well as spiritually profitable. We assured His Holiness that, thanks to our efficient priest-guide, it was both...

We mentioned to Our Holy Father how thrilled we were at the Byzantine Liturgy this morning. Did we have a good view, he asked? When we told him where we were, he laughed! It could not have been better, he said.

Cardinal Tisserant then introduced us to the other Cardinals present — there were ten of them, more cardinals than we had met in our entire lives before! — and to some of the bishops and monsignori present. We left soon afterward since we knew that they wanted to start their meeting. We thanked His Eminence, Cardinal Tisserant, who walked with us to the door, for permitting this rare visit with the Sacred Congregation of Rites...

After the meeting of the *Sacred Congregation of Rites,* the Holy Father came out to St. Peter's Square. A temporary altar had been erected between the two center columns at the entrance to the basilica . . . the Square was filled with thousands of people who had come to hear the Supreme Pontiff speak to the world—about peace . . .

"Peace!" said this great Pope, *"Who can estimate its worth and benefits?* Would that We could arouse a more fervent desire for it throughout the world, so that individuals and groups would henceforth consent to make the greatest and most personal sacrifices in order to protect, preserve and strengthen it." The Holy Father spoke with much feeling and emotion . . .

"How We wish men and nations would prefer it to the satisfactions of egotism and selfishness," the Pontiff continued. "How We hope that the pressure of world opinion will curb resistance and foolish stubbornness, make it necessary everywhere to settle even the sharpest disputes amicably and force the acceptance of arbitration and compromise, through which many irreparable evils can be avoided.

"We often hear the present age characterized—*not without a trace of complacency—*" he added, "as the era of the *'second technical revolution.'* In spite of the prospect of a better future which this characterization seems to imply, it is necessary to emphasize the permanency of suffering and of political and economic insecurity among the most fortunate peoples as well as in underdeveloped areas.

"The bitter experiences of the past century should be enough to explain this," he said emphatically. "Were not promises of a technically and economically perfect world made then as they are now? Did they not lead to cruel disillusion? The social upheavals brought about by the application of science in a spirit that was too often materialistic ruined the existing order without replacing it with a better or stronger one.

"The Church, on the other hand, has never lost sight of man's real needs and has dedicated herself to the mission of preserving the true stability of his existence. She knows that man's temporal destiny finds its sanction and fulfillment only in eternity. Without in any way denying the achievements of science and technology, she keeps them in their proper place and gives them their true meaning. They must serve man without upsetting the balance of all the relationships which make up the plan of his life—family, property, profession, community and state," the Pontiff asserted.

"To base the security and stability of human life only on an increasing quantity of material goods is to forget that man is primarily a spirit created in God's image. He is a being responsible for his actions and his destiny and capable of ruling

himself. He finds in these facts his highest dignity. *It is right to defend this freedom against outside restraints, against the threat of social systems which paralyze it and make it illusory.*

"But the very person who wages this battle," the Holy Father declared, "must realize that economics and technology are useful and even necessary forces so long as they are subservient to higher spiritual needs. They become harmful and dangerous only when they are given undue predominance and the dignity so to speak, of ends in themselves. It is the task of the Church to assure respect for this system of values and to subordinate the elements of material progress to truly spiritual goals...

"Slogans like *'national unity'* and *'social progress'* should not deceive us," he warned. "For militant materialism, *'peacetime'* means only a truce, a precarious truce during which it awaits the social and economic collapse of other peoples.

"That is why We are appealing to all who want peace and unity for mankind. With the help of God, such generous souls are becoming more numerous every day. They victoriously oppose their ideal of light and love to error and evil. Convinced that nothing solid can be built on sand, they rely on eternal truths that cannot be shaken by even the most categoric denials. For what human reason has long groped for, God in His goodness has shown to men in the person of His beloved Son. *'For He Himself is our peace.'*

"In His name and on behalf of peace for all humanity..." the Pontiff concluded, "We ask the most abundant divine favors for you and the countries you represent and give you Our Apostolic Blessing."

Wild cheers and tremendous applause followed this address of the Holy Father, who retired to the papal throne for the conclusion of the ceremonies. It took a long time before the applause and the cheering subsided. But while the Pope's words—and the applause—were still ringing in our ears, we thought again, what fortunate people we are, to have as wonderful a Pope as Pius XII to lead us in the right direction, to clarify the issues of the day, to guide the world...to peace! If *only* the world would listen... *if only ... the world ... would listen ...*

That evening, we got a copy of the Vatican's semi-official newspaper, *L'Osservatore Romano* — *The Roman Observer* — which reprinted the Holy Father's address, his *eloquent* address on *"Peace"* ... The paper also dedicated its entire front page to the *Pope of Peace* in honor of one of the Pontiff's anniversaries which was also celebrated that day...

This was the first time we had actually seen a copy of the Vatican newspaper. Our guide told us that a special courier delivers the first copy of *L'Osservatore* to Our Holy Father as soon as it is off the press... and, he informed us, every evening after dinner, the Pontiff spends almost an hour reading every news item and editorial in its pages...

We learned that 200,000 copies of the Vatican paper are printed every day. Copies go all over the world, not only to all the cardinals, chanceries and Catholic agencies, but to all the world leaders in London, Paris, Berlin, Washington, Lisbon, Barcelona — and even Moscow and other satelite capitals. But while *L'Osservatore* makes its way behind the iron and bamboo curtains, The Vatican also gets *Pravda* and other communist publications, the better to keep its fingers on the pulse of the Church's mortal enemy...

The editorial staff of *L'Osservatore* consists of some ten laymen, all prominent Vatican officials who are each experts in their particular fields, and each one personally chosen, or appointed, by the Holy Father. *Count Giuseppe Della Torre* has been editor of *L'Osservatore* for more than 30 years! He writes all the articles against communism himself, our guide said, and about 90% of all controversial pieces published in his paper. He is a bitter foe and a long-standing one, of communism, fascism, naziism and any other evil that oppresses, enslaves, tyrannizes or separates people from God, or from the practice of their religion.

Oddly enough, *L'Osservatore Romano* was founded at the request of *Pope Pius IX* around the year 1850 and he chose as its first editor a man by the name of *Marcantonio Pacelli* — the present pope's grandfather! He remained its editor until his death in 1902. He was then 102 years old!

It was certainly interesting to read the newspaper that Our Holy Father himself reads, and is, in a certain sense, responsible for. This copy will make a marvelous souvenir...

SECONDA EDIZIONE

NUMERO A OTTO PAGINE · LIRE 25

L'OSSERVATORE ROMANO

GIORNALE QUOTIDIANO POLITICO RELIGIOSO

UNICUIQUE SUUM · NON PRAEVALEBUNT

CITTA DEL VATICANO

Venerdì 12 Marzo 1954

SEGNI

AUSPICALI

Pius PP. XII

O MARIA
CHRISTIANORVM AMOR ET PRAESIDIVM
IN VOTA VBIQVE VOCATA TERRARVM
PIVM XII PONT. MAX.
PATREM NOBIS
SOSPITEM QVAM DIVTISSIME SERVA
PROVIDVM SERVA IN HISCE TEMPORVM FLVCTIBVS
NOBIS NAVARCHVM

H. TONDINI

After Mass and breakfast the next morning, we assembled in St. Peter's
Square. Our priest-guide wanted us to be present when the Supreme

making it an article of faith which must be accepted by every member of the Catholic Church. This was to be one of those rare, historical moments when the Pope speaks "*ex Cathedra*"—from the chair...

It was a good thing that we came early, because we were right up in front and behind us were masses of people. Noble and Swiss and Palatine Guards stood all around us when the Holy Father came, as well as many cardinals, bishops, monsignori and priests. As always, many Religious with their very colorful habits stood out in the throng around the square.

Our guide told us that the man on the Holy Father's right was *Nicola Cardinal Canali*, President of the Commission charged with the administration of Vatican City, and Grand Penitentiary. To the Pontiff's left stood *Giovanni Mercati*, Librarian and Archivist of the great Vatican Library.

On either side of the Vicar of Christ, we again noticed the colorful ostrich-plumed *flabellum*

... The two silver and gold inlaid microphones, our guide whispered, were gifts from the members of *Italian Catholic Action*.

In proclaiming this dogma, Pope Pius XII became the second Pontiff in the Church's history personally to make an infallible pronouncement. The first being Pius IX who promulgated the dogma of the *Immaculate Conception* in the year 1854.

The Holy Father was going out to *Castel Gandolfo* this afternoon, so we went out there early to see him arrive. Our guide had arranged for us to see the Holy Father before leaving for home this evening.

On the way out there, our priest-guide told us that *Castel Gandolfo* has been a papel residence since about 1600. It is located on a mountain overlooking the *Lake of Albano,* which is almost a thousand feet above sea level and happens to be — he said — the crater of an extinct volcano!

The name of *Castelgandolfo* comes from the *Gandolfi* family who came from Genoa to live here, in the twelfth century; afterwards, their castle passed to the *Savelli* family. It was acquired by the Holy See after that and the pope's summer palace was designed by *Maderna* and built for *Pope Urban VIII* in 1629. It was restored in 1933 when the observatory was added and is now combined with the gardens of the *Barberini* villa which used to belong to the *Emperor Hadrian*. Later, father told us, we'll take a look in at the Observatory if we have time.

The Holy Father's residence is 400 feet above *Lake Albano* which is fed by subterranean springs. Near the papal palace is the church of *St. Thomas of Villanova* which was designed by *Bernini* — we'll pass it on our way...

After a long, uphill climb, we finally reached *Castelgandolfo,* and took our place with the hundreds of people already lining the sides of the road where Our Holy Father will pass by... Soon, we saw it — there it was — the car bringing the Supreme Pontiff to *Castel Gandolfo*...the people waved white and yellow papal flags and shouted *"Viva il Papa! Viva il Papa! Viva...!"* Some people threw flowers in the path of the car.

The Holy Father blessed the people as he passed by... he was *always* blessing the people...that's the picture of the Holy Father I shall take away with me...

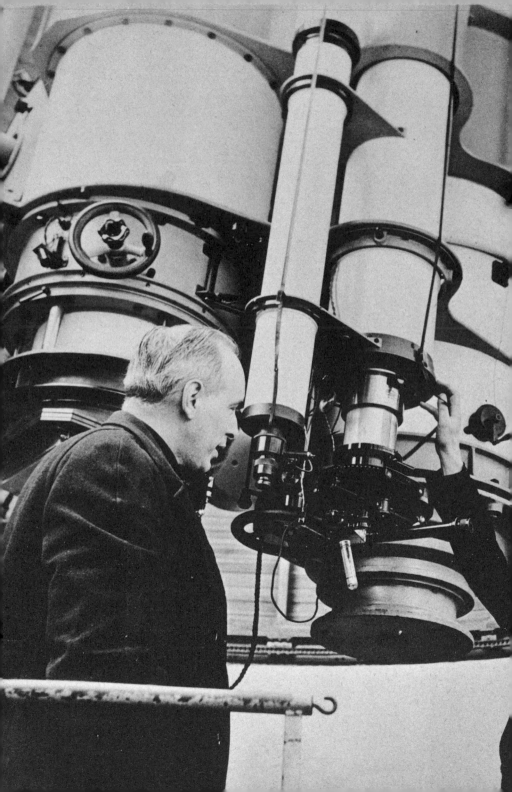

Since we had some time before our final audience with the Holy Father, our guide suggested that we visit the new Observatory here at Castel Gandolfo...

The Papal Observatory, father told us, was established by *Pope Gregory XIII* in 1582. The two towers are still located at Vatican City and we did remember seeing them there. But electrical interference hampered the workings of the delicate instruments and the Observatory was moved to Castel Gandolfo which is about 16 or 17 miles southeast of Rome...

We met *Brother Matthew Timmers* who was one of the members of the Observatory Staff. *Father Walter Miller, S.J.* of New York was visiting the Observatory also. We listened as Brother Timmers explained how he tracked a new comet which was named after him — *Timmer's Comet!* The telescope he was handling was the one used to track and log the new comet. It was a tremendous instrument!

Photography of the stars, Brother told us, is a major activity here, and they have more than 10,000 pictures on file! *Which is a tremendous amount of pictures,* we commented. *But just a drop in the bucket when you think of the billions upon billions of stars there are in the heavens,* replied Brother Timmers.

While he was showing us around the Observatory, he asked us if we knew anything about *Betelgeuse.* We confessed that we never even heard of *Betelgeuse.*

Well, Brother said, *Betelgeuse* is one of the stars in the constellation we call *Orion,* in fact it is a star of the first magnitude — located in the upper left hand corner of the rectangular shaped constellation. *Betelgeuse is so large,* he said, *that* the complete movement of the earth around the sun, with both of these bodies at their present distance apart, could take place *inside* Betelgeuse! It has a diameter of 290,000,000 miles! Yet, to our eyes, it is *just another star in the night sky...*" This aroused my interest so much that I resolved to learn more about these stars when I got back home...

At last it was time for our final appointment with the Holy Father. Ushered in past the ever-present Swiss Guards, we were greeted informally and cordially by the Supreme Pontiff himself. He asked us many questions about our visit, our impressions; he asked if we had seen Michelangelo's beautiful statue of *Moses* ... and the sculptor's famous *Pieta* ...

We told the Holy Father about some of the things that had impressed us, about the ceremonies, about *St. Peters*. What we didn't tell him was that HE had impressed us more than anything or anyone else! His kindness, his compassion for people, his interest in the poor, the sick, the people suffering behind the iron curtain ... I wanted to say these things, but it would have embarrassed him.

I did say that his talk yesterday on *"Peace"* was most inspiring. He was glad we thought so and asked us to pray constantly for peace; peace for nations, for families, for individuals — peace for the whole world!

We thanked His Holiness finally, for all that he had done to make so many things possible during this pilgrimage and we also expressed our gratitude to His Eminence, *Cardinal Tisserant* for all his help. We also told the Pontiff what a tremendous and invaluable help our priest-guide had been to us. Could we have the Holy Father's blessing now, we asked? Gladly, he replied, he would bless us, our families, all our relatives, our friends and all those with whom we worked. He left no one out ... we knelt down and he blessed us ...

Then he gave us another medallion. We told His Holiness that he had already given us one like this before, but he insisted that we take this also. We accepted gratefully.

As we came out into the hallway, the Holy Father explained that he had been asked to bless this painting of *St. Pius X* which was going to the Marist chapel at *Cendrole* near Riesi in *Sicily*. We watched as he blessed the painting and we left shortly afterward ... filled with great joy and new courage ... *so much had been given to us on this pilgrimage* ... so many blessings and graces and spiritual gifts ... *how much better we ought to be now,* I thought, as we drove back to Rome ...

"After all this ... we really ought to be saints ourselves ... !" I said to our priest-guide.

"Or at least ... *try* to be ..." he replied.

On our way back to our hotel... our pilgrimage to *The Vatican* over... we examined this latest medallion given us by the Supreme Pontiff... one of the medallions struck to commemorate his pontificate. On the reverse side were some of the Saints canonized by Pius XII...

I could recognize *Mother Cabrini* and *Catherine Labouré*. I think the other nun on the left is *Mary Euphrasia Pelletier*. Among the men, I thought I recognized *Grignon de Montfort; Don Cafasso* — a contemporary and friend of Don Bosco; *John de Britto, S.J.; Nicholas of Flue,* a hermit; and *Bernardo Realini, S.J.*

Our priest guide informed us that a check of the records going back as far as *Pope Sixtus V* who died in 1590, revealed that, with one exception, *Pope Pius XII had canonized more Saints than any other pope since that time* ... over 35 ... Pope Pius IX raised 42 to sainthood...

Since the year 993, father said, there have been approximately 250 solemn proclamations of sainthood...

Holding the medallion in my hands, and realizing that it had been given to me by Pope Pius XII himself...thinking back over the past few days and all the wonderful experiences we had...the ceremonies we saw... the Masses we offered right from the basilica of St. Peter's...the people we met...the prayers we offered...somehow, I felt a great sense of elation...of joy...of consolation...

I felt secure in the knowledge that all these things were part of a great heritage that came down to us —- of this day and age — from the hands of Christ Himself...it was all part of His Providential design that the Church should be His Voice, His Hands, His Feet, His very Self even...healing the sick, comforting the afflicted...preaching the message of redemption to all men in all the centuries and ages down to the end of time...and here, in The Vatican, was *His Other Self*, the *Vicar of Christ*...whom we had seen, and to whom we had spoken...

It was an experience I shall never forget...

Back at the Hotel, a member of our pilgrimage who was the photographer, got some of his film back from the Fotoshop. These were a few of the shots he had taken of the Holy Father ... quite good we thought ...

I bought some picture post cards of *St. Peter's* and put Vatican postage stamps on them to send to the family and many friends back home as mementos of our pilgrimage here ... Perhaps you may want to put someone's name on this "card" and mail *The Vatican Picture Book* to them ... as a souvenir of *your* "Picture Pilgrimage" ...

OUR PILGRIMAGE ENDS... ◇ ◇ ◇

Also waiting for us at the Hotel was a beautiful *Papal Blessing* obtained for us by our good priest friend and guide. And so... we come to the end of our pilgrimage... *may the things we have seen and learned keep our hearts and minds always lifted up to God...*

And since this has been only a *"Picture Pilgrimage"*... we want to clarify a few things before we take our leave.

In order for us to make this *"Picture Pilgrimage"* possible; in order for us to make it a *spiritual* experience rather than just *another picture book* on The Vatican, we have taken many liberties with the *sequence* of events, with some of the events themselves, and also with some of the people in our pictures. All the photographs were arranged so that there would be some continuity from scene to scene... from day to day...

Naturally, we never met *Cardinal Tisserant,* nor did His Eminence arrange for our pilgrimage, which was not necessary since it was merely *pictorial!* But we thought it would be a good device for getting the eminent Dean of the College of Cardinals *into* our "pilgrimage"... Nor could the Holy Father humanly participate in as many ceremonies as we placed him in. The events and ceremonies of many years were condensed into the period of a few days simply to make it possible for us to simulate a *real* pilgrimage, and make it *spiritually profitable.*

Our *"priest-guide"* is only a figment of the editor's imagination... and while we hope this fact will not prove too great a disillusionment, it was necessary to invent such a person in order to *"take us from scene to scene and from day to day."*

Aside from these contrived situations and people, the information given with each picture is basically correct. Much research went into the text in order for it to be as accurate as possible. But in any case, this is not supposed to be either a text-book on *The Vatican,* nor a guide book. We took pains to avoid making it sound technical or encyclopedic. It was simply an attempt to give the reader a *"Picture Pilgrimage"* that he could enjoy and benefit from spiritually. *If that has been done, then we thank God for it!*

If you wish to drop us a note letting us know how you liked this kind of *"Picture Pilgrimage"* — we would be most happy to hear from you...

The Editor

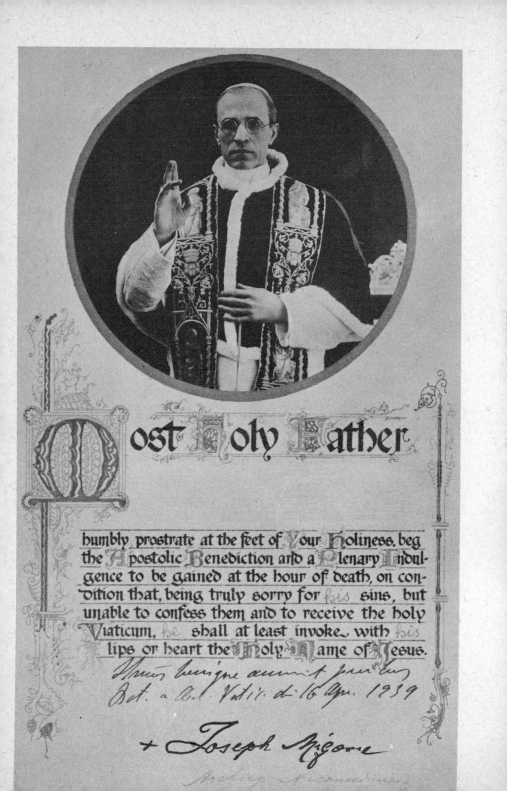

Most Holy Father

humbly prostrate at the feet of Your Holiness, beg
the Apostolic Benediction and a Plenary Indul-
gence to be gained at the hour of death, on con-
dition that, being truly sorry for his sins, but
unable to confess them and to receive the holy
Viaticum, he shall at least invoke with his
lips or heart the Holy Name of Jesus.

Preces benigne annuit pour leur
Dat. a Vat. Vat. V. d. 16 Apr. 1939

† *Joseph Migone*

Archiep. Nicomedien.